The Little Big Book of Classical MYTHOLOGY In the Visual Arts

Cover: Sandro Botticelli, *The Birth of Venus*, Uffizi Gallery, Florence

pp. 2–3: Felice Fiani, *Dispute Between Achilles and Agamemnon*, Palazzo Milzetti, Faenza

pp. 4–5: Alexandre Cabanel, *The Birth of Venus*, Musée d'Orsay, Paris

pp. 6–7: Diego Vélazquez, *VTriumph of Bacchus*, Prado, Madrid

p. 9: Sandro Botticelli, *Pallas and the Centaur*, Uffizi Gallery, Florence

pp. 10–11: Jean-Auguste-Dominique Ingres, *Jupiter and Thetis*, Musée Granet, Aix-en-Provence

The Little Big Book of Classical Mythology in the Visual Arts
was created and produced by McRae Books Srl
Borgo Santa Croce, 8 – Florence (Italy)
www.mcrabooks.com, info@mcraebooks.com

Publishers: Anne McRae, Marco Nardi
Project Managment: Gabriella Greco
Translation: Brian Eskenazi
Graphic Design: Marco Nardi
Layouts: Los Tudio
Editing: Chiara Gini, Barbara Caria
Repro: Puntoeacapo

ISBN-13: 978-88-6098-036-6
ISBN-10: 88-6098-036-4

Printed and bound in China, by C&C Offset Printing

The Little Big Book of Classical

MYTHOLOGY

In the Visual Arts

Roberto Carvalho de Magalhåes

McRAE BOOKS

Contents

Introduction

The classical texts from which we know Greek mythology were only a tiny part of a much larger literary output, most of which has been lost forever. Even so, these few sources provide a rich, detailed, complex, and often contradictory view of the myths, which change depending on the author and the century in which they were written. In the subsequent Roman tradition, the gods and goddesses of the Greek mythological universe became identified with the local deities of the Italian peninsula and were associated with new deeds and attributes. In 391 AD, all pagan rituals were outlawed in the Roman Empire and the ancient temples were abandoned, along with the mythological view of the creation of the world, humanity, cities, and states. New Christian ideas about the origins of the world and mankind replaced the ancient worldview. Even though many classical texts were preserved and copied by monks during the Middle Ages, it was not until the 15th century that they were rediscovered and systematically studied and translated (especially in Florence). This gave impetus to a philosophical and cultural movement, known as Neoplatonism, that sought to resolve Christian views and morality with the philosophy and mythology of the ancient Greeks and Romans. Ever since then, Greek mythology, with its seemingly inexhaustible wealth of stories, symbols, and ideas, has been a constant companion of the so-called Western world, both in its surviving, original literary forms, and as the spark for new literary, artistic, and theatrical works, and movies.

As well as the ancient literary sources, from Homer's epics, to Hesiod's poems and the tragedies of Aeschylus, Sophocles,

Agostino di Duccio
Florence, 1418–Perugia, c. 1481

Saturn
Relief
c. 1456

Marble
Tempio Malatestiano, Rimini

and Euripides, we have inherited a large number of archeological finds—statues, ceramics, mosaics, cameos, and wall paintings—that bring the myths to life visually. With the advent of Christianity and the subsequent Edict of Theodosius in 391, mythological subjects were abandoned by artists and replaced with new Christian ones. For about a thousand years, the Greek and Roman gods and heroes were banned from sculpture, frescoes, and paintings.

The renewed interest in the ancients, from the 15th century onward, had important consequences for art, which, as well as emulating the style of classical statuary and architecture, brought mythological subjects back into circulation. Among the earliest—and most surprising—examples of works of art with mythological subjects in the 15th century are a bas-relief by Agostino di Duccio depicting *Cronus* (Saturn) (Rimini, Tempio Malatestiano) dating to about 1456, and Antonio del Pollaiolo's paintings of *Hercules and the Hydra* (Florence, Uffizi Gallery,) of about 1460, and *Apollo and Daphne* (London, National Gallery), of about 1475.

However, art is not merely illustration and beyond the more or less recognizable subject matter in a work of art, every artist expresses his or her own ideas. This means that the delicate rendering of Dionysus' journey of the 6th century BC by the vase painter Exekias, has little in common with Caravaggio's fleshy *Bacchus* (Dionysus). In the first, the forms are slender and musical, almost in contradiction with the violent and impassioned episode they are thought to represent. In the latter, the image is animated by the contrast of light and shadow, and the almost tangible objects, such as the basket of fruit and the wine carafe or the cup that the god appears to be offering us. Notwithstanding the shared protagonist, the two works have very different points of view: Exekias seems to have sacrificed the storyline to the aim of creating a rhythmic and harmonious composition; Caravaggio has set before us an adolescent in flesh and blood, clearly dedicated to pleasure, with the light playing on the objects around him.

A book on mythology in art is therefore both a challenge and an opportunity. The challenge consists in making the mythological subjects used by the artists—which are by their very nature quite intricate—clear and comprehensible. The opportunity, on the other hand, lies in being able to show long sequences of works, from ancient art to modern, with similar themes produced by artists in different times and places which, despite their shared subject matter, almost immediately reveal the personal styles of the artists and the diverse tendencies of the epochs and cultural areas in which the works were produced.

The aim of this book is not to provide an exhaustive overview of all the myths—a task that mythological dictionaries can better fulfill (although not without some difficulty)—but rather to explain the myths and legends that have been most often represented by artists across time. Because it is art that guides us in fulfilling this task, the absence of some gods

Mars and Venus
Detail from the House of Venus and Mars, Pompeii
2nd century BC

Wall painting
National Archeological Museum, Naples

and heroes is due to their relative lack of popularity with sculptors and painters. Vice versa, the ample treatment given to some deities and heroes, such as Aphrodite and Heracles, is because they have been so often represented in art.

In the hope of inspiring a passion for mythological themes and for their use in art, and, indeed, for art itself, where appropriate we have quoted the classical sources of the myths and legends. This places them in a direct relationship with the works of art shown, allowing the reader to find the episodes in the original texts and to compare them with the paintings, sculptures, and mosaics that have made use of them. A brief dictionary at the end of the volume includes the names of the gods, goddesses, and heroes who, although present in many works, have not been included in the brief introductions to each chapter.

Remembering, with Picasso, that "art washes away from the soul the dust of everyday life" and that "If there were only one truth, it wouldn't be possible to paint a hundred variations on the same subject," we hope that this book will inspire further reading in the fields of mythology and art.

William Blake
London, 1757–1827

Homer
c. 1800

Tempera on canvas
15 ¾ x 33 in
(40 x 84 cm)
Manchester City
Art Gallery,
Manchester

Félix Boisselier

Damfal, Le Val de Meuse, 1776–Rome, 1811

Homer Singing with his Lyre

Early 19th century

Oil on canvas
24 x 18 in (61 x 46 cm)
Private collection

Theogony

Francisco Goya
Fuendetodos, Saragozza, 1746–Bordeaux, 1828

Saturn Devouring his Son
1820–1823

Mural transferred to canvas
57 ½ x 32 ⅔ in
(146 x 83 cm)
Prado, Madrid

The first Greek writer to produce a systematic and detailed narrative of the creation of the world, the birth of the gods, and their rise to power, was Hesiod, who lived in the 8th century BC. In his poem *Theogony* he tells how "in the beginning was Chaos;" in the original Greek chaos meant "yawn." Chaos was followed by Gaia (Earth), Tartarus (a region believed to be below the earth), Eros (later known as Cupid), Erebus, and Night. Gaia then gave rise to Uranus (the Heavens), the mountains, and Pontos (the sea). Mating with Uranus, Gaia gave birth to the twelve Titans, including Cronus, Rhea, and Iapetos, to the Cyclopes (creatures with a single eye in the middle of the forehead), and to three monstrous creatures with fifty heads and a hundred arms each, known as the Hecatoncheires. The decision by Uranus to imprison the Cyclopes and the Hecatoncheires deep within the body of their mother Gaia (the Earth), never allowing them to see the light of day, so enraged Gaia that she tried to turn her other children, the Titans, against their father. Only Cronus would listen to her, and when, according to the poem (*Theogony*, 176–177), "huge Uranus, desiring love and bringing night with him, came to Gaia and stretched out, covering her completely," Cronus cut off his father's genitals with a sickle and threw them over his shoulder. The drops of blood fell on Gaia and fertilized her and she gave birth to the Giants. The genitals landed in the sea and produced a white foam (*aphros* in Greek) from which Aphrodite (known to the Romans as Venus) was born.

In this way, Cronus took the place of his father. From his union

Rhea Deceiving Cronus
Attic vase
c. 460 BC
Ceramic
h. 17 in (43. 6 cm)
Louvre,
Paris

with his sister Rhea came some of those who constituted the second generation of the gods and some of the twelve deities of Mount Olympus. Gaia and Uranus had, however, put Cronus on guard against his own children, telling him that he was destined to be dethroned by his son. In order to prevent this, as soon as Rhea gave birth, Cronus devoured his own children and thus swallowed Demeter, Hestia, Hera, Hades, and Poseidon. Desperate with sorrow, and pregnant again, Rhea begged her parents to find a way for her to give birth in secret and to guarantee the survival of the new child. Gaia and Uranus sent her to Crete, where she gave birth to Zeus. In place of the child, Rhea gave Cronus a rock swaddled like a baby, which he devoured, thinking it was his newborn son.

So Cronus did not succeed in avoiding his fate. On reaching maturity, Zeus somehow forced Cronus to regurgitate first the rock and then, one by one, his brothers and sisters, who returned to life. Later there was a great battle between Zeus and Cronus. Allied with Zeus were his reborn brothers and sisters as well as the Cyclopes and the three Hecatoncheires, liberated by him from the imprisonment imposed on them by Uranus and Cronus. On the side of Cronus were his powerful brothers, the Titans, with the exception of Oceanus. One of their descendants, Prometheus, the son of Iapetus and Clymene, gave his help to Zeus, while his brother Atlas fought alongside Cronus. Grateful to Zeus for freeing them, the Cyclopes gave him lightning bolts and thunder, and the Hecatoncheires hurled tremendous boulders at the Titans. Zeus defeated his father, sent the Titans down to Tartarus, the

Athena Taking Alcyoneus by the Hair

Detail of eastern frieze from the Altar of Zeus and Athena, Pergamon

First half of the 2nd century BC

Marble
c. 78 ¾ x 98 ½ in
(c. 200 x 250 cm)
Pergamonmuseum, Berlin

deepest part of the Underworld, and became the ruler of the gods on Mount Olympus. In Greek mythology this war is known as the Titanomachy.

In order to consolidate his reign, Zeus still had to deal with the rebellion of the Giants and the anger of Typhon, the youngest son of Gaia. Even though he mentions the Giants, Hesiod does not tell the story of their struggle against the second generation of the gods, to seek revenge for the defeat of the Titans. But the episode is told by others, for example by the Roman author Ovid, in his *Metamorphoses*, written much later and the probable source for Renaissance painters such as Giulio Romano and Perino del Vaga who treated the theme. Immense creatures, with snakes instead of hair and the bodies of dragons in place of legs, the Giants launched their attack on Olympus as soon as they were born. They were quasi-immortal and could only be killed by a god and a mortal working together. Heracles, the legendary mortal son of Zeus, came to the aid of the Olympian gods and agreed to help them defeat their enemies.

In his *Theogony*, on the other hand, Hesiod narrates that when Zeus defeated the Titans, from the relationship between Gaia and Tartarus came Typhon, a terrible creature with one hundred serpent heads shooting flames from its eyes. The writer Apollodorus, in his *Library* (I,6), adds that Typhon was so frightening that when he attempted to scale Mount Olympus the other gods fled to Egypt to hide themselves and took the shape of animals, leaving Zeus by himself. Typhon

Giulio Romano
Rome, c. 1499–
Mantua, 1546

The Fall of the Giants
Detail
1532–1534

Fresco
Palazzo Tè,
Sala dei Giganti,
Mantua

was so gigantic that his heads often bumped against the stars. After a tremendous battle in which the earth was turned upside down, Zeus made him flee and, when the monster tried to reach Sicily, Zeus hurled Mount Etna on top of him (Apollodorus, *Library*, I,6). The eruptions of Etna's volcano are said to come from either the flames emitted by Typhon, the lightning bolts with which Zeus defeated him, or the forge of Hephaestus.

At the center of the myth of the creation of the world and of the birth and rise to power of the gods is the story of Prometheus, one of the most popular figures in all of classical mythology. His story is linked to that of the human race, which he helped against the oppression of Zeus. Although other sources speak of Prometheus as the creator of humanity (Apollodorus, *Library*, I,7; Ovid, *Metamorphoses*, I, 82), in Hesiod's *Theogony* he appears above all as the one who fools the ruler of the gods in order to benefit mankind. Prometheus stole fire from Mount Olympus and gave it to humans. In this way, he drew the wrath of Zeus on himself and on the human race. To punish Prometheus, the ruler of Olympus bound him to a rock (according to some sources, in the Caucasus) and every day sent an eagle to eat his liver, which grew back again during the night. In order to end this torture, Heracles chased off the eagle and freed Prometheus. According to a blending of the narrative in various versions, including *Theogony* and *The Works and Days* by Hesiod and *Natural History* by Pliny, the punishment for men was the creation of Pandora, the first woman, molded in form like the goddesses. Created with the

Nicolas-Sébastien Adam
Nancy, 1705–Paris, 1778

Prometheus Bound
1762

Marble
h. 44 ¾ in (114 cm)
Louvre, Paris

participation of all the gods, she was given many qualities such as beauty, grace, and the power of persuasion. At the same time, Hermes made telling lies part of her character, along with cunning, and Hera added curiosity. Pandora was sent to Epimetheus, the brother of Prometheus, with a jar sealed with a lid like a wedding gift. Overcome with curiosity, she opened the jar, pouring out on mankind all the evils that it contained. It was only Hope that could not escape the jar before Pandora reclosed it. In this way ended the "golden age" of man, who up until that time had lived in a state of permanent happiness. The similarity of this myth with that of Eve in the Old Testament is obvious. And, perhaps, it is no accident that the French painter Odilon Redon gives us a representation of Pandora very close to the Judeo-Christian Eve without especially emphasizing the mythic jar of calamities, but in a luxuriant multi-colored garden that reminds us of the earthly paradise.

In the history of art, the myths connected to the creation of the world, the birth of the gods, and the confirmation of Zeus as the ruler of Olympus circulated in various ways. Obviously, every episode and personality is the subject of at least one representation on a krater, a calyx or a Greek vase, and there are also many reliefs and sculptures in the round, both Greek and Roman, which depict them. Even though they reappear in the art of the Renaissance, after a long absence from the advent of Christianity to the very end of the 14th century, these myths were superseded by others in the preferences of artists and patrons. In the myth of the birth of Zeus, we can compare

Dante Gabriel Rossetti
London, 1828–Birchington-on-Sea, 1882
Pandora
1869
Chalk on paper
c. 39 ½ x 28 ½ in
(100.6 x 72.7 cm)
The Faringdon Collection Trust, Buscot Park, Oxfordshire

the "classic" versions, balanced and composed, of an Attic krater from the 5th century BC (Paris, Louvre) and of a Roman high relief from about 160 AD (Rome, Capitoline Museum), with the representation of the delivery by Rhea to Cronus of a rock instead of the newborn Zeus. A marble relief by Agostino di Duccio from about 1456 (Rimini, Tempio Malatestiano) shows Cronus seizing one of his children, while a painting from the 1600s and one from the 1800s, by Rubens and Goya respectively, put the accent on the cruel and terrible aspects of the myth of Cronus devouring his children for fear of being dethroned. There are spectacular depictions of the punishment inflicted by Zeus on Atlas after the battle of the Titans, such as the *Farnese Atlas* from the 1st–2nd century AD (Naples, National Archeological Museum) and the painting by Guercino from 1645–46 (Florence, Museo Bardini) that seems to be inspired by the antique sculpture mentioned above. More frequent are the depictions of Prometheus. A beautiful calyx from Laconia from 550 BC (Vatican City, Vatican Museums), shows the tortures of Prometheus and Atlas, while Prometheus as the creator of mankind is depicted in a Roman fresco on a tomb on the Via Ostiense (Ostia, Museum). Stories about Prometheus were taken up again in the early 1500's by the Florentine painter Piero di Cosimo and continued to inspire artists up to the late 19th century, when the French painter Gustave Moreau completed a series of works, including paintings, watercolors, and sculptures, taking this unhappy friend of mankind for their subject.

"FOR HE LEARNED FROM GAIA AND STARRY URANUS
THAT HE WAS DESTINED TO BE OVERCOME BY HIS OWN SON,
STRONG THOUGH HE WAS, THROUGH THE CONTRIVING OF GREAT ZEUS.
THEREFORE HE KEPT NO BLIND OUTLOOK,
BUT WATCHED AND SWALLOWED DOWN HIS CHILDREN:
AND UNCEASING GRIEF SEIZED RHEA."

(HESIOD, , 463-467)

Peter Paul Rubens
Siegen, 1577–Antwerp, 1640

Saturn Devouring his Son

1636–1637

Oil on canvas
71 x 34 ¼ in (180 x 87 cm)
Prado,
Madrid

Theogony

Giulio Romano

Rome, c. 1499–
Mantua, 1546

The Fall of the Giants

Detail showing Olympus
1532–1534

Fresco of the vault
c. 236 x 275 in
(600 x 700 cm)
Palazzo Tè,
Sala dei Giganti,
Mantua

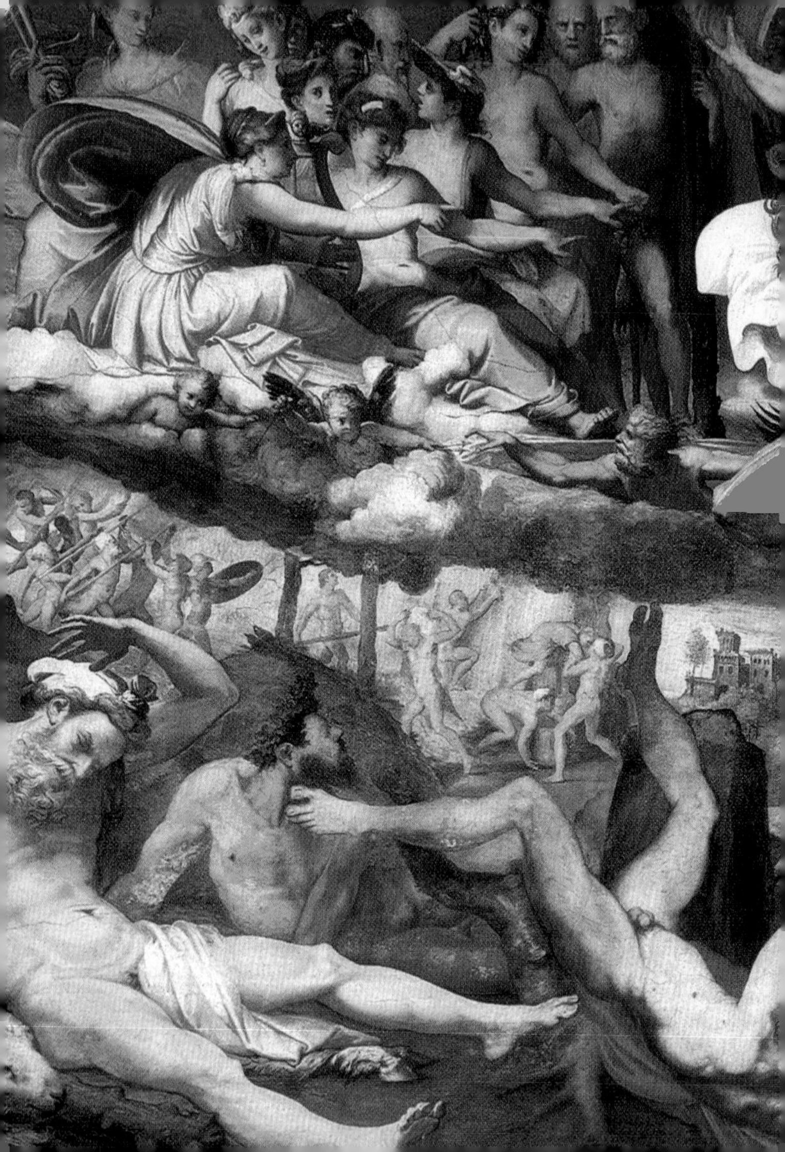

Cesare Rossetti

Active in Rome between the end of 16th century and the first half of the 17th century

The Battle between Gods and Giants

16th century

Oil on panel
34 ¾ x 26 in (88.2 x 66 cm)
Private collection

pp. 42–43

Perin del Vaga

Florence, c. 1501–Rome, 1547

The Fall of the Giants

c. 1527

Fresco
Palazzo Doria di Fassolo, Genoa

Odilon Redon

Bordeaux, 1840–Paris, 1916

The Cyclops

c. 1914

Oil on canvas
26 x 20 ¾ in (65.8 x 52.7 cm)
Kröller-Müller Museum,
Otterlo

"AND ATLAS THROUGH HARD CONSTRAINT
UPHOLDS THE WIDE HEAVEN
WITH UNWEARYING HEAD AND ARMS,
STANDING AT THE BORDERS OF THE EARTH
BEFORE THE CLEAR-VOICED HESPERIDES..."

(HESIOD, *THEOGONY*, 517-520)

Farnese Atlas

Roman copy from a Greek original (Hellenistic period)
2nd century AD

Marble
h. 75 in (191 cm)
National Archeological Museum, Naples

pp. 52–53

The Legend of Prometheus

Sarcophagus from Pozzuoli

4th century AD

Marble
National Archeological Museum, Naples

Guercino (Giovanni Francesco Barbieri)

Cento, Ferrara, 1591–Bologna, 1666

Atlas

1645–1646

Oil on canvas
50 x 39 ¾ in (127 x 101 cm)
Museo Bardini, Florence

Prometheus

Second half of the 3rd century AD
Greco-roman mosaic of Shahba
107 x 130 ¾ in
(272 x 332 cm)
National Museum, Damascus

pp. 56–57

Piero di Cosimo

Florence,
1461–1521

The Legend of Prometheus

c. 1520

Oil on panel
26 ¾ x 47 ¼ in
(68 x 120 cm)
Alte Pinakothek,
Munich

Piero di Cosimo

Florence,
1461–1521

The Legend of Prometheus

c. 1515

Oil on panel
25 x 45 ½ in
(64 x 116 cm)
Musée des
Beaux-Arts,
Strasbourg

pp. 60–61

Guercino (Giovanni Francesco Barbieri)
Cento, Ferrara 1591 –Bologna, 1666

Prometheus Animates Man with Fire

c. 1616

Fresco
78 ¾ x 59 in (200 x 150 cm)
Cassa di Risparmio, Cento, Ferrara

Dirck van Baburen
Utrecht, c. 1595–1624

Prometheus Being Chained by Vulcan

1623

Oil on canvas
79 ½ x 72 ½ in (202 x 184 cm)
Rijksmuseum, Amsterdam

Prometheus and Atlas

Laconian kylix from Cerveteri

560–550 BC

Ceramic
h. 5 ½ in,
diam. 8 in
(h. 14 cm,
diam. 20.2 cm)
Museo Gregoriano Etrusco,
Vatican City

Gioacchino Assereto

Genoa, 1600–1649

The Torture of Prometheus

c. 1625–1649

Oil on canvas
32 ½ x 27 ¼ in
(83 x 69.5 cm)
Museum of the Charterhouse, Douai

66

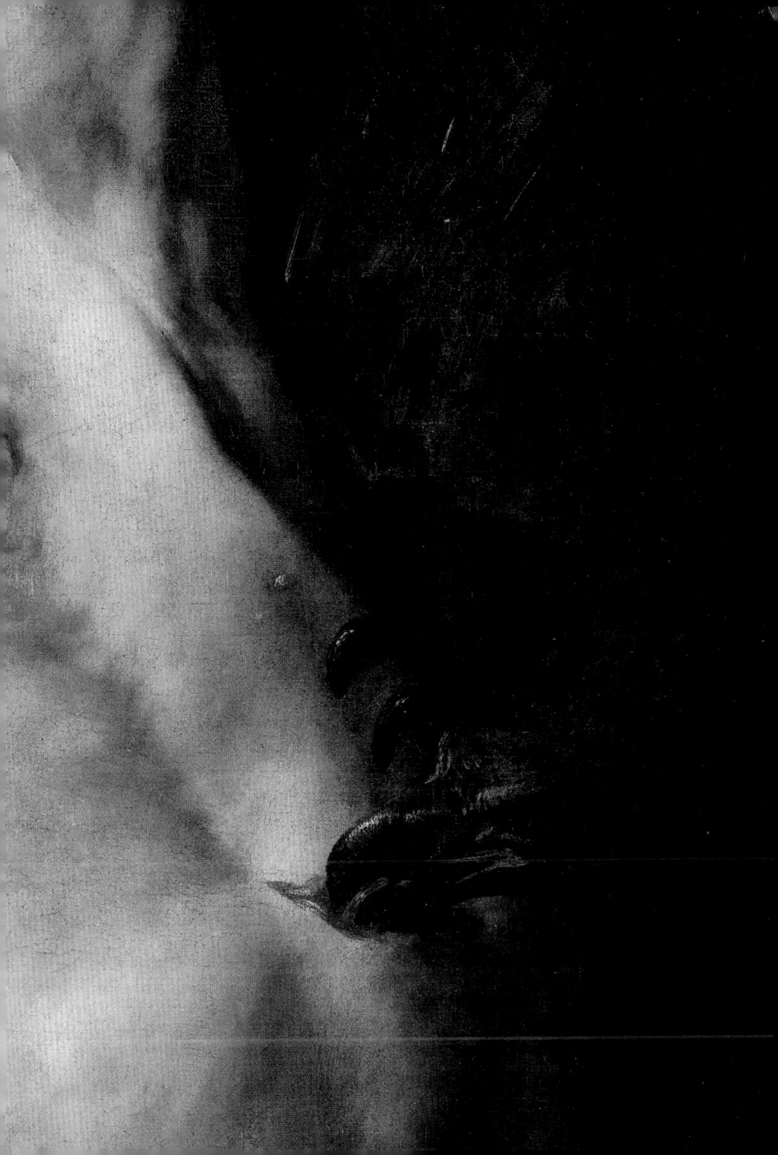

Luca Giordano

Naples, 1634-1705

Prometheus

c. 1660

Oil on canvas
73 ¼ x 52 in
(186 x 132 cm)
Szépmúveszeti
Museum,
Budapest

"AND READY-WITTED PROMETHEUS HE
BOUND WITH INEXTRICABLE BONDS,
CRUEL CHAINS, AND DROVE A SHAFT
THROUGH HIS MIDDLE,
AND SET ON HIM A LONG-WINGED EAGLE,
WHICH USED TO EAT HIS IMMORTAL LIVER;
BUT BY NIGHT THE LIVER GREW AS MUCH
AGAIN EVERYWAY
AS THE LONG-WINGED BIRD DEVOURED IN
THE WHOLE DAY."

(HESIOD, *THEOGONY*, 521-525)

Gustave Moreau
Paris, 1826–1898

The Torture of Prometheus

1868

Oil on canvas
80 ¾ x 48 in (205 x 122 cm)
Musée Gustave Moreau,
Paris

Pierre Puvis de Chavannes
Lyon, 1824–Paris, 1898

Prometheus
detail
c. 1896

Oil on canvas
49 ½ x 24 ½ in
(126 x 62 cm)
The Barnes Foundation, Merion

72

pp. 74–75

Arnold Böcklin

Basel, 1827–San Domenico, Florence, 1901

Prometheus

1882

Oil on canvas
45 ½ x 59 in
(116 x 150 cm)
Collezione Barilla d'Arte Moderna, Parma

Group of Polygnotos

The Birth of Pandora

Attic krater

c. 450 BC

Ceramic
h. 19 in (48.2 cm)
Ashmolean Museum,
Oxford

pp. 78–79

Jean Cousin the Elder

Sens, Yonne, c. 1490–c. 1560

Eva Prima Pandora

c. 1550

Oil on panel
38 x 59 in
(97 x 150 cm)
Louvre,
Paris

Paolo Farinati

Verona, 1524–1606

Pandora Offers the Box to Epimetheus

16th century

Pen and ink and wash on paper
18 ¾ x 15 ¼ in
(48 x 38.8 cm)
Hamburger Kunsthalle, Hamburg

80

Theogony

"FOR THE VERY FAMOUS LIMPING GOD
FORMED OF EARTH
THE LIKENESS OF A SHY MAIDEN AS THE SON
OF CRONOS WILLED.
AND THE GODDESS BRIGHT-EYED ATHENA
GIRDED
AND CLOTHED HER WITH SILVERY RAIMENT,
AND DOWN FROM HER HEAD SHE SPREAD
WITH HER HANDS A BROIDERED VEIL,
A WONDER TO SEE;
AND SHE, PALLAS ATHENA, PUT ABOUT HER
HEAD LOVELY GARLANDS,
FLOWERS OF NEW-GROWN HERBS."

(HESIOD, *THEOGONY*, 570-577)

Sir Lawrence Alma-Tadema
Dronrijp, 1836–Wiesbaden, 1912

Pandora
1881

Watercolor on paper
c. 11 ¾ x 15 ¾ in (30 x 40 cm)
Royal Watercolour Society,
London

The Olympians

The victory by Zeus over Cronus and the Titans brought about the establishment of what may be called the council of the gods, or the twelve gods of Olympus. Zeus was the ruler. He took his sister Hera as a wife and from their union Ares (known to the Romans as Mars) was born. Hera, on her own and without mating with Zeus, produced Hephaestus (known to the Romans as Vulcan). Other offspring of Zeus, who had a liking for amorous conquest, were Apollo, Artemis, Athena, Hermes, and Dionysus. According to Homer, and contrary to what Hesiod says in his *Theogony*, even Aphrodite was born from an "extramarital" relationship on the part of the god (see the chapter on Aphrodite). With the exception of Dionysus, these divinities, together with Demeter, Hestia, Hera, and Poseidon (who along with Zeus were children of Cronus and Rhea and therefore his siblings), would be the rulers of Olympus and masters of the fates of mankind. Hades, another child of Cronus and Rhea, was the ruler of the Underworld and not one of the gods who lived on Olympus.

The gods of Olympus, besides having supernatural powers, also embodied the virtues and the faults of humans. They shared with humans such feelings as jealousy, envy, and a desire for revenge, as well as compassion. Pandora's famous jar, or box, mentioned in the preceding chapter, explains the hardships visited on the human race after Prometheus gave humans the fire stolen from Olympus. We should not forget that the evils contained in the box were placed there by those same gods. Thus the various alliances and feuds among the Olympians were the cause of the ups and downs of life

Cylindric Altar with Jupiter and the Gods of Olympus

Relief

Second half of the 1st century BC

Marble
h. c. 39 ¼ in (100 cm)
Museo Ostiense,
Ostia

Annibale Carracci
Bologna, 1560–Rome, 1609

Paris and Mercury
Detail of the gallery vault
1597–1600

Fresco
Palazzo Farnese, Rome

experienced by humans as well as the defeats and victories of the heroes. The gods use them as instruments of revenge and also protect them. This can be seen in the jealousy and the desire for revenge of Hera (known to the Romans as Juno). Continuously betrayed by her husband Zeus, she persecuted his lovers and their children. According to the myth, even the Trojan war had its far-off beginning in a dispute among three goddesses, Hera (Juno), Athena (Minerva), and Aphrodite (Venus) that was instigated by Eris, the goddess of strife. The deceitful Eris had not been invited to the wedding feast of Peleus and Thetis, so she sent a golden apple as a gift to the one who was "most beautiful." In order to be judged most beautiful and to win the golden apple, Aphrodite promised Paris, the Trojan prince who had been named to judge the contest by Zeus, the love of Helen. Paris, with the help of Aphrodite, abducted Helen, who was the wife of Menelaus, and this was the cause of the Trojan war. According to some authors, Helen was not abducted but ran off voluntarily. In his tragedy *Andromache*, Euripides even casts doubt on the honesty of Helen, putting these words addressed to Menelaus in the mouth of Peleus, the father of Achilles: "...Helen, who fooled Zeus, the protector of matrimony, and left Sparta in order to enjoy herself elsewhere with some young boy. And for her you have assembled thousands of Greeks and sent them against Troy? Instead of going to war you should have disowned Helen, seeing what she was like. Better if you had left her there and given a gift to the Trojans for having taken her." Aphrodite would protect the Trojans, among whom was Aeneas, the son she had with Anchises, but she also had to confront the anger

Raphael (Raffaello Sanzio) and assistants
Urbino, 1483–Rome, 1520

Psyche Received on Olympus
Cycle of Cupid and Psyche
c. 1518

Fresco. Villa Farnesina, Rome

of Hera and Athena, who were helping the Greeks. The greatest epic poems of Classical Antiquity are all connected to the Trojan war: the *Iliad* and the *Odyssey* of Homer and the *Aeneid* of Virgil.

Among the oldest depictions of the council of the gods are the friezes from 440 BC that decorated the Parthenon in Athens. The subject appeared again in the Renaissance in a fresco by Raphael and his school in the Villa Farnesina in Rome (1515–17).

Phidias

Athens, c. 490–c. 430 BC

Zeus, Hera, and Nike

Relief from the Parthenon, eastern frieze

c. 438–432 BC

Marble
h. c. 39 ¼ in
(100 cm)
British Museum, London

92

Phidias

Athens, c. 490–
c. 430 BC

Hermes, Dionysus, Demeter, and Ares

Relief from the Parthenon, eastern frieze

c. 438–432 BC

Marble
h. c. 42 in (106 cm)
British Museum, London

94

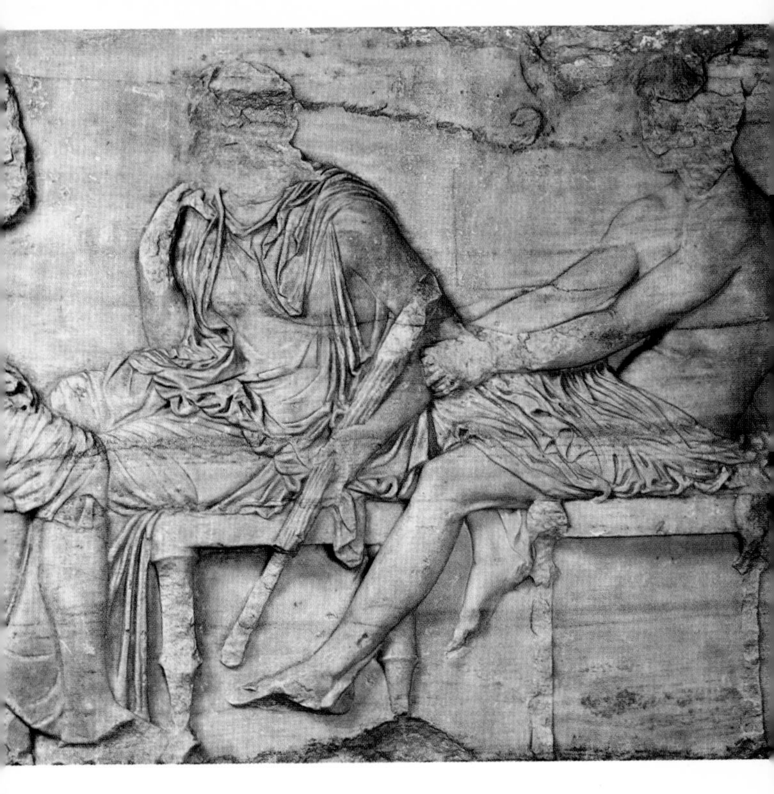

Andrea Mantegna

Isola di Carturo, Padua, 1431–Mantua, 1506

Parnassus

c. 1497

Tempera on canvas
63 x 75 ½ in
(160 x 192 cm)
Louvre,
Paris

Giulio Romano

Rome, c. 1499–
Mantua, 1546

Mount Olympus

1525–1535

Fresco
Palazzo Tè,
Loggia del
Giardino Segreto,
Mantua

pp. 100–101

Dosso Dossi

Ferrara,
c. 1489–1542

Jupiter, Mercury, and Virtue

1529

Oil on canvas
44 x 59 in
(112 x 150 cm)
Kunsthistorisches
Museum,
Vienna

Veronese (Paolo Caliari)

Verona, 1528–
Venice, 1588

Olympus

c. 1560–1563

Fresco
Villa Barbaro,
Sala dell'Olimpo,
Maser, Treviso

Hendrik
de Clerck

Brussels,
c. 1570–1630

The Banquet of the Gods

study
Oil on panel
20 ½ x 29 ¾ in
(52.5 x 75.7 cm)
Private collection

104

pp. 106–107

Cornelis van Poelenburg
Utrecht, c. 1586–1667

The Banquet of the Gods

c. 1630

Oil on copper
15 x 19 ¼ in
(38 x 49 cm)
Mauritshuis, The Hague

Giuseppe Maria Crespi (Lo Spagnolo)

Bologna, 1665–1747

Olympus

Vault fresco, detail

1699–1701

Fresco
344 x 330 ½ in
(875 x 840 cm)
Palazzo Pepoli
Campogrande,
Bologna

Andrea Appiani
Milan, 1754–1817

Olympus
1806

Oil on canvas
17 ¾ x 53 ½ in
(45 x 136 cm)
Pinacoteca
di Brera,
Milan

pp. 114–115

Bartolomeo di Giovanni

Florence, 1483–1511 (?)

The Marriage of Thetis and Peleus

c. 1490–1500

Oil on panel
c. 16 ½ x 59 in
(42 x 150 cm)
Louvre, Paris

Luigi Sabatelli

Florence, 1772–Milan, 1850

Olympus

c. 1850

Fresco
Palazzo Pitti,
Florence

Manuel Niklaus Deutsch

Bern, c. 1484–1530

The Judgement of Paris

1517–1518

Tempera on canvas
87 ¾ x 63 in
(223 x 160 cm)
Kunstmuseum,
Basel

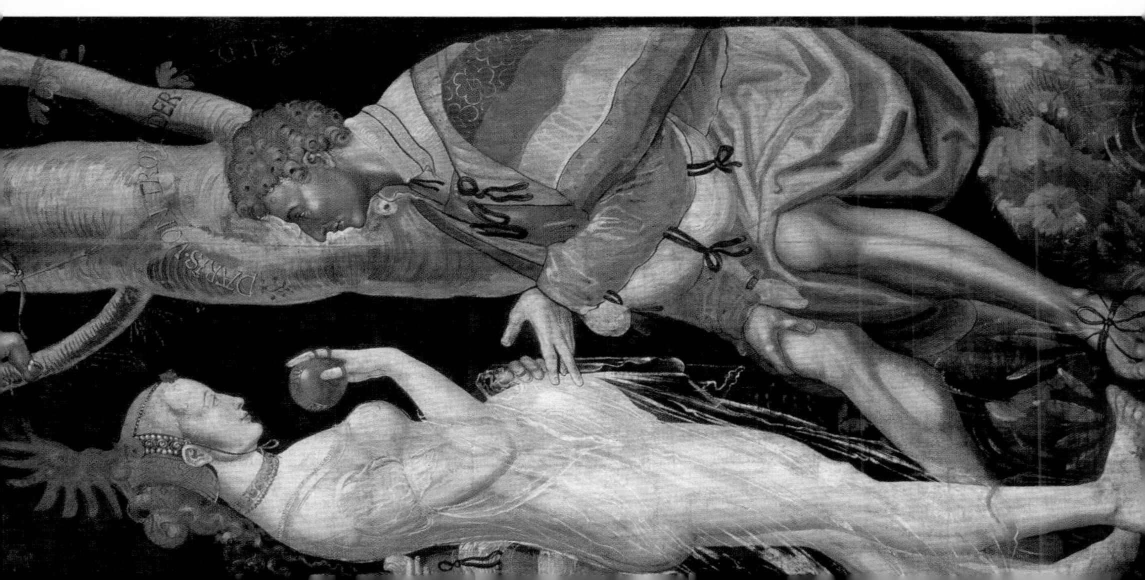

Lucas Cranach the Elder

Kronach, 1472–Weimar, 1553

The Judgement of Paris

1527

Oil on panel
19 ½ x 15 in
(50 x 38 cm)
Statens Museum for Kunst, Copenhagen

118

121

Hendrik de Clerck

Brussels,
c. 1570–1630

Denys van Alsloot

Malines, c. 1570–
Brussels, 1628

The Judgement of Paris

Second half of the 16th century

Oil on panel
29 ½ x 38 in
(75 x 97 cm)
Schloß Mosigkau Museum,
Dessau

German school

The Judgement of Paris

17th century

Marble
Hermitage,
St. Petersburg

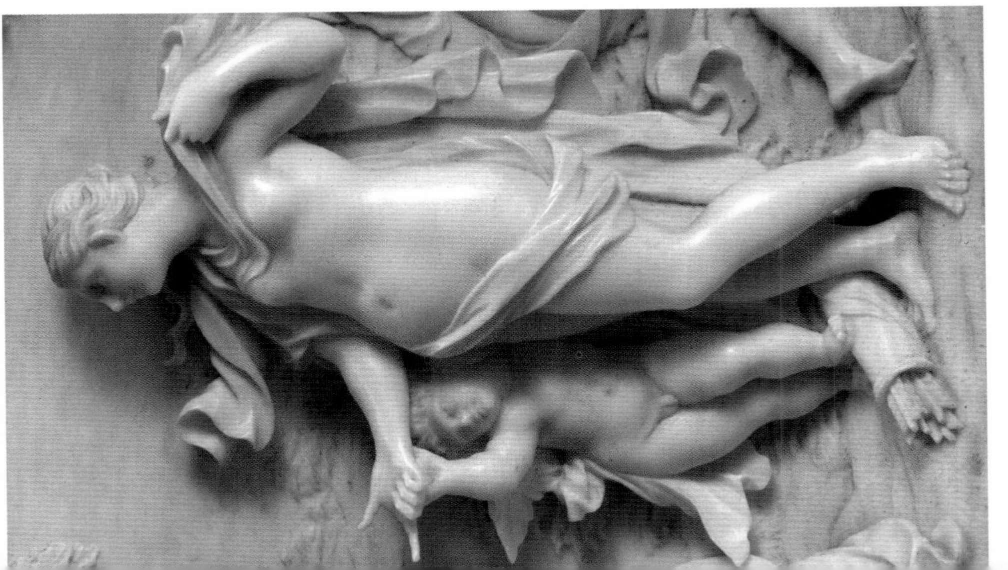

pp. 124–125

David Rossi
1741–1827

The Judgement of Paris
Detail
1827

Fresco
Villa Loschi Zileri dal Verme, Vicenza

Guido Reni

Bologna,
1575–1642

The Abduction of Helen

1626–1629

Oil on canvas
99 ½ x 104 in
(253 x 265 cm)
Louvre,
Paris

Giovanni Battista Piazzetta

Venice, c. 1683–1754

The Abduction of Helen

c. 1718

Oil on canvas
92 ¾ x 70 ¾ in
(235.5 x 180 cm)
Musée Granet,
Aix-en-Provence

"NOW CYPRIS HELD OUT MY BEAUTY,
IF AUGHT SO WRETCHED DESERVES THAT NAME,
AS A BRIDE BEFORE THE EYES OF PARIS,
SAYING HE SHOULD MARRY ME;
AND SO SHE WON THE DAY;
WHEREFORE THE SHEPHERD OF IDA LEFT HIS STEADING,
AND CAME TO SPARTA, THINKING TO WIN ME FOR HIS BRIDE."

(EURIPIDES, *HELEN OF TROY*, 27-30)

Evelyn De Morgan
London, 1855-1919

Helen of Troy
1898

Oil on canvas
38 1/2 x 18 3/4 in (98 x 48 cm)
De Morgan Centre,
London

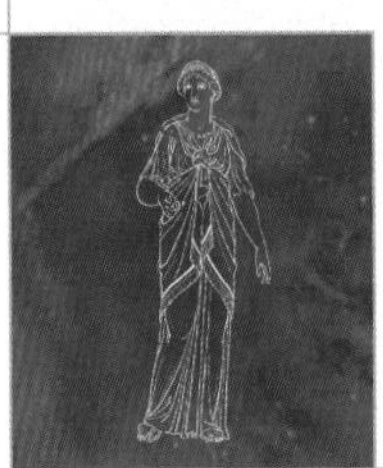

Head of Juno

Roman copy of a 5th-century BC Greek work depicting Hera, from the Ludovisi Collection, Rome

1st–2nd century AD

Marble
Palazzo Altemps,
Anticamera delle Quattro Stagioni,
Rome

Giovanni Ambrogio Figino
Milan, c. 1548–1608

Jupiter, Io, and Juno

Second half of the 16th century

Oil on canvas
83 x 57 in
(211 x 145 cm)
Pinacoteca Malaspina, Pavia

pp. 136–137

Jan Gotlief Glauber-Myrtill
1656–1703

Zeus and Hera

17th century

Oil on panel
18 ¼ x 22 ¾ in
(46.5 x 58 cm)
Art Museum of Estonia, Kadriorg Palace,
Tallinn

Veronese (Paolo Caliari)
Verona, c. 1528–Venice, 1588

Juno Bestowing her Gifts on Venice

1553–1555

Oil on canvas
250 x 57 ¾ (635 x 147 cm)
Palazzo Ducale
Sala del Consiglio dei Dieci,
Venice

The Triumph of Neptune

Floor from Wadi Blibane House

3rd century AD

Roman mosaic
43 ¼ x 70 ¾ in
(110 x 180 cm)
Musée Archéologique, Sousse

Mabuse (Jan Gossaert)

Maubeuge, c. 1478–Middelburg, 1532

Neptune and Amphitrite

1516

Oil on canvas
74 x 48 ¾ in (188 x 124 cm)
Staatliche Museen, Gemäldegalerie,
Berlin

pp. 144–145

Jacob Jordaens

Antwerp,
1593–1678

Neptune Creates the Horse

c. 1640–1650

Oil on canvas
51 ½ x 26 ¼ in
(131 x 67 cm)
Palazzo Pitti,
Galleria Palatina,
Florence

"POSEIDON, THE GREAT GOD, MOVER OF THE EARTH AND FRUITLESS SEA,
GOD OF THE DEEP WHO IS ALSO LORD OF HELICON AND WIDE AEGE.
A TWO-FOLD OFFICE THE GODS ALLOTTED YOU, O SHAKER OF THE EARTH,
TO BE A TAMER OF HORSES AND A SAVIOR OF SHIPS!"

(*HOMERIC HYMNS*, XXII,
"HYMN TO POSEIDON," 1-5)

Lambert-Sigisbert Adam

Nancy, 1700–Paris, 1759

Neptune

1737

Marble
h. 33 ½ in (85 cm)
Louvre,
Paris

Correggio (Antonio Allegri)

Correggio, Reggio Emilia, 1489–1534

Venus with Mercury and Cupid (The School of Love)

c. 1525

Oil on canvas
61 ¼ x 36 in (155.6 x 91.4 cm)
National Gallery,
London

"ARES, EXCEEDING IN STRENGTH, CHARIOT-RIDER,
GOLDEN-HELMED, DOUGHTY IN HEART, SHIELD-BEARER,
SAVIOR OF CITIES, HARNESSED IN BRONZE,
STRONG OF ARM, UNWEARYING, MIGHTY WITH THE SPEAR,
O DEFENCE OF OLYMPUS..."

(*HOMERIC HYMNS*, VIII, "HYMN TO ARES" 1-3)

Diego Velázquez

Seville, 1599–Madrid, 1660

Mars

c. 1640

Oil on canvas
70 ½ x 37 ½ (179 x 95 cm)
Prado,
Madrid

Diana the Huntress

3rd–4th century AD

Mosaic floor
200 ¾ x 200 ¾ in
(510 x 510 cm)
Musée National
du Bardo,
Le Bardo

Artemis and Atteone

1st–2nd century AD

Roman mosaic
Soueida Museum,
Soueida

pp. 156–157

François Clouet

Tours, c. 1510–
Paris, 1572

The Bath of Diana

1560

Oil on panel
53 ½ x 77 ¼ in
(136 x 196.5 cm)
Musée des
Beaux-Arts,
Rouen

Jan Bruegel
the Elder

Brussels, 1568–
Antwerp, 1625

**Diana and
the Nymphs**

c. 1620–1625

Oil on panel
22 x 37 in
(55.8 x 94.1 cm)
Private collection

Diana

c. 1700

Tapestry
Schloss Museum,
Gobelin Hall,
Jever

pp. 162–163

Titian (Tiziano Vecellio)

Belluno, c. 1490–
Venice, 1576

Diana and Actaeon

1556–1559

Oil on canvas
35 ½ x 81 ½ in
(90.3 x 207 cm)
National Gallery of
Scotland, Edinburgh

Jacob Jordaens
Antwerp, 1593–1678

Diana and Actaeon

1650

Oil on panel
20 ¾ x 28 ¾ in
(53 x 73 cm)
Gemäldegalerie
Alte Meister,
Dresden

Zeus

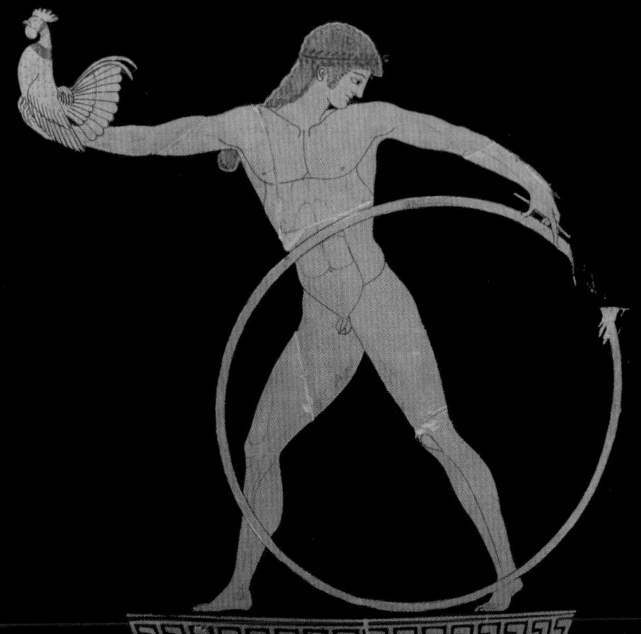

Cristoforo De Predis (attributed to)
From *De Sphaera* manuscript, p. 6v

Jupiter with Pisces and Sagittarius

Second half of the 15th century

Miniature
c. 9 ½ x 7 in
(24.5 x 17 cm)
Biblioteca Estense, Modena

Lord of heaven and earth, father of gods and men, Zeus was worshiped at cult sites all over ancient Greece. To the Romans, he was known as Jove, or Jupiter, with a temple dedicated to him on the Capitoline, one of the seven hills of ancient Rome. For both Romans and Greeks, Zeus had the same divine attributes. For the ancient Greeks, he was the god responsible for maintaining order and justice in the world, and he was the judge in disputes among the various gods on Mount Olympus. Moreover, he was the embodiment of destiny, which he defended against the whims and rebellions of the other gods and heroes. In this sense, he dispensed both good and evil. Zeus was directly or indirectly involved in most of the mythological stories and was very often depicted in art. The divine attributes with which he is often identified are the lightning bolt and the eagle. Zeus is often seen with them in ancient sculpture and pottery, as a ruler or ready to hurl a lightning bolt or accompanied by an eagle. It was said that the lightning bolt was given to him as a gift by the Cyclopes, while the eagle was associated with Zeus because it is the most powerful of birds, the ruler of the skies because of its keen sight.

Despite his position as judge and guarantor of order in the world, even Zeus was not immune to whims and caprices, and his "transgressions" were mostly amorous ones. To the despair of Hera, his wife, Zeus not only made love to other goddesses, but also to a long list of mortal women. From these unions various gods and heroes were born. As Hesiod tells us in his *Theogony*, Apollo and Artemis were the result

Pontormo (Jacopo Carrucci)
Pontorme, Empoli, 1494–Florence, 1556

Leda and the Swan
1512–1513
Oil on panel
21 ½ x 15 ¾ in
(55 x 40 cm)
Uffizi Gallery, Florence

of the love between Zeus and Leto (daughter of the Titans Coeus and Phoebe). Other writers tell us that when Hera learned that Leto was pregnant, she was so jealous that she would not allow any village or city on earth to welcome Leto or provide a place for her to give birth (Apollodorus, *Library*, I). In this way she made Leto wander the earth until she came to the island of Ortygia, a wretched strip of land that seemed to float above the water. After Apollo and Artemis, children of Zeus and future gods of Olympus, were born, Apollo was grateful to the place that had welcomed his mother and anchored the island to the seabed, renaming it Delos, "the sparkling place," which gave birth to the god of light. Through a trick, Zeus seduced the mortal woman Alcmene, who conceived Heracles. Zeus also made love to Semele, who conceived Dionysus. Falling in love with Danae, he possessed her by taking the form of a shower of gold and from this union came Perseus. Very often, in order to satisfy his amorous desires, Zeus would transform himself into an animal. In this way, he could hide from Hera and her tricks and satisfy his desires in secret. In order to mate with Leda, the wife of Tyndareus, he came to her in the form of a swan. The various ancient authors tell different versions of the story, but according to one by Euripides, after sleeping with Zeus, Leda produced one egg, or perhaps two, from which came the twins Castor and Pollux as well as Helen and Clytemnestra. While Apollonius of Rhodes (*Argonautica*, I, 146) only refers to Castor and Pollux, as being children of Leda, Apollodorus (*Library*, III) says that Pollux and Helen came from Leda's union with Zeus and that Castor and

Zeus and Ganymede

c. 470 BC

Terracotta
h. 42 ½ in
(108 cm)
Olympia Museum, Olympia

Clytemnestra were the children of Tyndareus, who also slept with her that same night. Another story tells how Zeus saw the young and beautiful Europa, the daughter of the Phoenician king, playing on the banks of a river and transformed himself into a white bull, kneeling in front of her. Overcoming her fear, Europa caressed the animal and mounted it. The bull ran off with her on its back and crossed the sea, arriving in Crete. There it mated with her and she gave birth to Minos, Sarpedon, and Rhadamanthus. Zeus then caused her to marry Asterion, the king of Crete, who adopted her sons.

The amorous attentions of Zeus were not only directed at women. In the mountains surrounding the city of Troy lived a boy of incomparable beauty. His name was Ganymede and, according to Homer, he was the son of the Trojan king Tros and looked after his herds. Ganymede was carried off and taken to Mount Olympus, where he was cup-bearer for the gods. There are different versions of the story among the ancient authors. In ancient art there are depictions of an anthropomorphic Zeus carrying the boy to Mount Olympus (e.g. an Attic cup in the Spina Museum and the terracotta sculpture in the Archeological Museum at Olympia, both from the 5th century BC), while the version most often illustrated in the art of the 1500s and later is that narrated by Apollodorus (*Library*, III, 9) and Ovid (*Metamorphoses*, X, 155) which shows Zeus, overcome by the beauty of Ganymede, transforming himself into an eagle and carrying the boy up to the heavens.

Tintoretto (Jacopo Robusti)
Venice, 1518–1594

Danae
1555–1560

Oil on canvas
56 x 71 ½ in
(142 x 182.5 cm)
Musée des Beaux Arts, Lyon

The amorous escapades of Zeus would become a common subject in art after the 1500s. Correggio dedicated an entire series of paintings to them, including the *Danae* in Rome at the Galleria Borghese, *Leda and the Swan* in Berlin at the Staatliche Museum, and *Jupiter and Io* and the *Rape of Ganymede*, both in Vienna at the Kunsthistorisches Museum. Other painters took up these same subjects and, choosing additional examples from the many available to us, we can mention paintings from diverse eras, styles, and geographical areas, including the *Danae* by the Flemish painter Jan Gossaert, known as Mabuse, in Munich at the Alte Pinakothek, as well as the same subject by Titian in Naples at the Museo di Capodimonte, and by Orazio Gentileschi at the Cleveland Museum of Art. Rembrant painted a *Rape of Europa*, now at the Getty Museum in Los Angeles, and a *Rape of Ganymede*, at the Gemäldegalerie in Dresden.

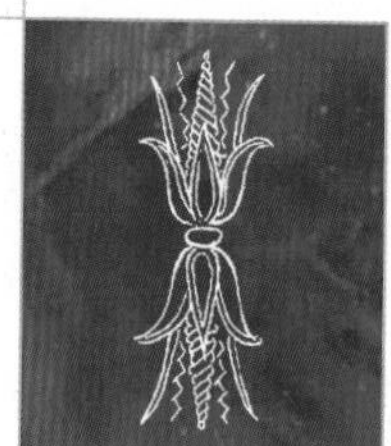

Artemision Zeus (or Poseidon)

c. 460 BC

Bronze
h. 6 ft 10 ¾ in (209 cm)
National Archeological Museum,
Athens

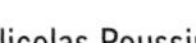

Nicolas Poussin
Les Andelys, 1594
–Rome, 1665

The Nurture of Jupiter
1630

Oil on canvas
37 ¾ x 47 in
(96.2 x 119.6 cm)
Dulwich Picture
Gallery,
London

Felice Giani

San Sebastiano Curone, Alessandria, c. 1758–Rome, 1823

Jupiter Nurtured by the She-goat Amalthea

Oil on canvas
13 x 16 ¼ in
(33 x 41 cm)
Private collection, Bologna

Correggio (Antonio Allegri)

Correggio, Reggio Emilia, 1489–1534

Danae

c. 1531

Oil on canvas
63 ¼ x 76 in
(161 x 193 cm)
Galleria Borghese, Rome

Francesco Primaticcio

Bologna, 1504-Paris, 1570

Danae

c. 1535-1540

Fresco
100 x 39 ¾ in
(254 x 101 cm)
Gallery of Francois I, Chateau de Fontainebleau

pp. 186–187

Rembrandt Harmenszoon van Rijn

Leiden, 1606–Amsterdam, 1669

Danae

1636

Oil on canvas
72 3/4 x 79 3/4 in
(185 x 202.5 cm)
Hermitage,
St. Petersburg

Leda and the Swan

Roman

Cameo in agate and onyx
1 x ½ in
(2.7 x 1.5 cm)
Farnese Collection,
National Archeological Museum,
Naples

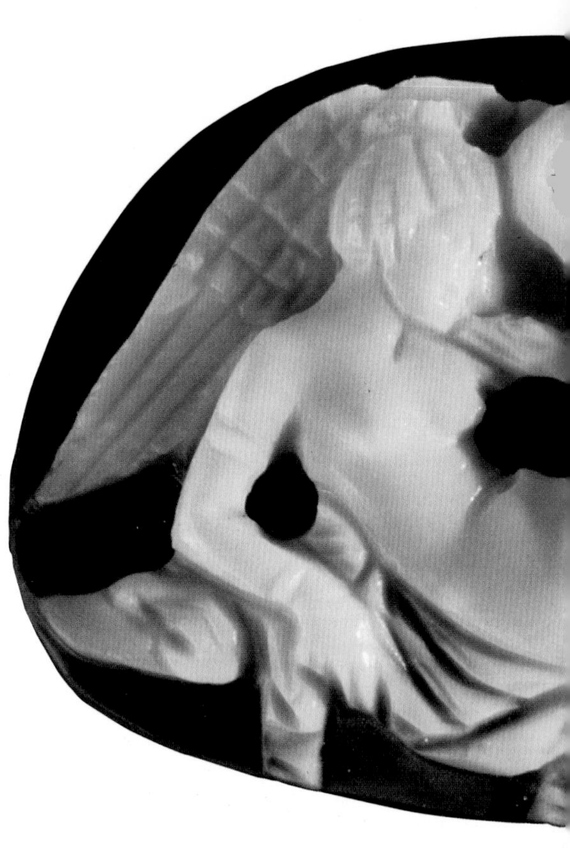

“BUT ZEUS IN THE FORM OF A SWAN CONSORTED WITH LEDA,
AND ON THE SAME NIGHT TYNDAREUS COHABITED WITH HER;
AND SHE BORE POLLUX AND HELEN TO ZEUS,
AND CASTOR AND CLYTAEMNESTRA TO TYNDAREUS.”

(APOLLODORUS, *LIBRARY*, III, 10, 7)

pp. 192–193

Correggio (Antonio Allegri)
Correggio, Reggio Emilia, 1489–1534
Leda and the Swan
c. 1531
Oil on canvas
59 ¾ x 75
(152 x 191 cm)
Gemäldegalerie, Staatliche Museen, Berlin

Cesare da Sesto
Sesto Calende, Varese, 1477–Milan, 1523
Leda and the Swan
Copy from the original by Leonardo da Vinci
c. 1505–1510
Oil on panel
27 ¼ x 29 in (69.5 x 73.7 cm)
Wilton House, Collection of the Earl of Pembroke,
Salisbury

Bartolomeo Ammannati

Settignano, Florence, 1511–Florence, 1592

Leda

c. 1535

Marble
h. 19 ½ in (50 cm)
National Museum of the Bargello, Florence

"NOT KNOWING THAT SHE PREST THE THUNDERER,
SHE PLACED HER SELF UPON HIS BACK,
AND RODE OVER FIELDS AND MEADOWS,
SEATED ON THE GOD.
HE GENTLY MARCHED ALONG,
AND BY DEGREES LEFT THE DRY MEADOW,
AND APPROACHED THE SEAS;
WHERE NOW HE DIPS HIS HOOFS AND WETS HIS THIGHS,
NOW PLUNGES IN, AND CARRIES OFF THE PRIZE."

(OVID, *METAMORPHOSES*, II)

Europa on the Bull
Metope from Selinus temple
c. 560 BC

Limestone
Regional Archeological Museum, Palermo

Liberale da Verona

Verona, c. 1445–c. 1529

The Rape of Europa

c. 1470

Oil on panel
15 1/4 x 46 1/2 in
(39 x 118 cm)
Louvre,
Paris

pp. 200–201

Jean Cousin
the Young
(attributed to)

Sens, 1522–Paris,
c. 1594

**The Rape
of Europa**

c. 1576

Oil on panel
34 ½ x 55 in
(88 x 140 cm)
Musée des Beaux-
Arts, Blois

Rembrandt Harmenszoon van Rijn
Leiden, 1606–Amsterdam, 1669

The Rape of Europa
1632

Oil on canvas
24 1/2 x 30 3/4 in
(62.2 x 77 cm)
The J. Paul Getty Museum, Malibu

Veronese
(Paolo Caliari)
Verona, 1528–1588

**The Rape
of Europa**

1576–1580

Oil on canvas
94 ½ x 119 ¼ in
(240 x 303 cm)
Palazzo Ducale,
Sala dell'Anticollegio,
Venice

204

206–207

François
Boucher
Paris, 1703–1770

**The Rape
of Europa**

1747

Oil on canvas
63 x 16 in
(160 x 193 cm)
Louvre,
Paris

Berlin Painter

Ganymede
Bell Krater
500–490 BC

Ceramic
h. 13 in, diam. 13 in
(h. 33 cm,
diam. 33 cm)
Louvre,
Paris

pp. 208-209

Gustave Moreau
Paris, 1826–1898

The Rape of Europa
1869

Oil on panel
10 ¼ x 16 ½ in
(26 x 42 cm)
Musée d'Orsay,
Paris

Painter of Pentesilea

The Rape of Ganymede

Attic kylix

c. 470 BC

Ceramic

Museo Spina,

Ferrara

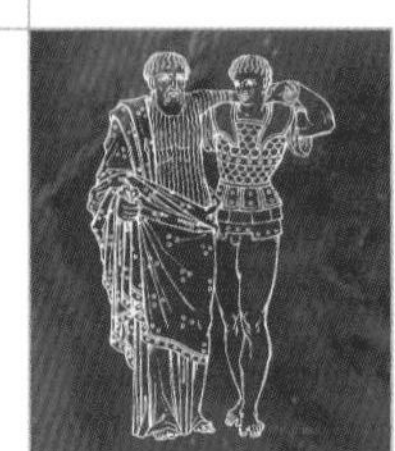

Correggio (Antonio Allegri)

Correggio, Reggio Emilia, 1489-1534

The Abduction of Ganymede

c. 1534

Oil on canvas
64 ¼ x 29 in (163.5 x 74 cm)
Kunsthistorisches Museum,
Vienna

Lelio Orsi
Novellara,
1511–1587

The Rape of Ganymede
1546

Fresco transferred to canvas
116 in
(295 cm)
Galleria Estense, Modena

Zeus

"THE KING OF GODS ONCE FELT THE
BURNING JOY,
AND SIGHED FOR LOVELY GANYMEDE OF TROY.
LONG WAS HE PUZZLED TO ASSUME A SHAPE
MOST FIT, AND EXPEDITIOUS FOR THE RAPE;
A BIRD'S WAS PROPER, YET HE SCORNS TO
WEAR
ANY BUT THAT WHICH MIGHT HIS
THUNDER BEAR.
DOWN WITH HIS MASQUERADING WINGS
HE FLIES,
AND BEARS THE LITTLE TROJAN TO THE SKIES
WHERE NOW, IN ROBES OF HEAVENLY PURPLE
DREST,
HE SERVES THE NECTAR AT THE ALMIGHTY'S
FEAST,
TO SLIGHTED JUNO AN UNWELCOME GUEST."

(OVID, *METAMORPHOSES*, X)

Benvenuto Cellini (attributed to)
Florence, 1500–1571

Ganymede
c. 1570

Bronze
h. 23 ½ in (60 cm)
National Museum of the Bargello,
Florence

Peter Paul Rubens

Siegen, 1577–Antwerp, 1640

The Abduction of Ganymede

1611–1612

Oil on canvas
80 x 80 in
(203 x 203 cm)
Palace Schwarzenberg, Vienna

Rembrandt Harmenszoon van Rijn

Leiden, 1606–Amsterdam, 1669

The Rape of Ganymede

1635

Oil on canvas
67 ¼ x 51 in (171 x 130 cm)
Gemäldegalerie Alte Meister,
Dresden

"VERILY WISE ZEUS CARRIED OFF GOLDEN-HAIRED GANYMEDE
BECAUSE OF HIS BEAUTY,
TO BE AMONGST THE DEATHLESS ONES
AND POUR DRINK FOR THE GODS IN THE HOUSE OF ZEUS,
A WONDER TO SEE, HONORED BY ALL THE IMMORTALS
AS HE DRAWS THE RED NECTAR FROM THE GOLDEN BOWL."

(*HOMERIC HYMNS*, V, "HYMN TO APHRODITE," 202-206)

Anton Raphael Mengs (attributed to)
Aussig, Boemia, 1728–Rome, 1779

Jupiter and Ganymede
c. 1758–1760

Fresco transferred to canvas
70 1/4 x 54 in (178.7 x 137 cm)
Palazzo Barberini,
Galleria Nazionale d'Arte Antica,
Rome

227

Gustave Moreau

Paris, 1826–1898

Jupiter and Semele

c. 1890

Oil on canvas
58 ½ x 43 ¼ in
(149 x 110 cm)
Musée Gustave Moreau,
Paris

Tintoretto (Jacopo Robusti)
Venice, 1518–1594

Jupiter and Semele

1541–42

Oil on panel
60 ¼ x 52 ¼ in
(153 x 133 cm)
Galleria Estense, Modena

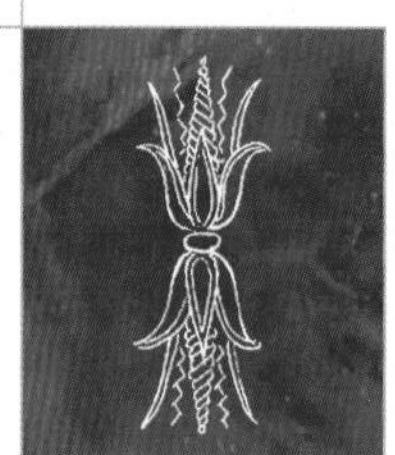

Sebastiano Ricci
Belluno, 1659–Venice, 1734

Jupiter and Semele

1695

Oil on canvas
71 1/4 x 59 1/2 in (181 x 151 cm)
Uffizi Gallery,
Florence

"... 'BUT YOU CAN MAKE HIM PAY FOR THIS,
PROFOUND MIND OF OLYMPUS!
LEND THE TROJANS POWER,
UNTIL THE ACHAEANS RECOMPENSE MY SON
AND HEAP NEW HONOR UPON HIM!'
SO SHE SPOKE, AND ZEUS SAT FOR A WHILE
SILENT, AND WITHOUT A WORD,
BUT THETIS STILL KEPT FIRM HOLD OF HIS
KNEES,
AND BESOUGHT HIM A SECOND TIME ..."

(HOMER, *ILIAD*, 508-513)

Jean-Auguste-Dominique Ingres
Montauban, 1780–Paris, 1867

Jupiter and Thetis

1811

Oil on canvas
128 ¾ x 102 ¼ (327 x 260 cm)
Musée Granet,
Aix-en-Provence

pp. 236-235

Jacopo Amigoni

Naples, 1682–
Madrid, 1752

Jupiter and Callisto

1730

Oil on canvas
24 ¼ x 30 in
(62 x 76 cm)
Hermitage,
St. Petersburg

Correggio (Antonio Allegri)

Correggio, Reggio Emilia, 1489–1534

Jupiter and Io

c. 1530

Oil on canvas
64 ¼ x 29 in (163.5 x 74 cm)
Kunsthistorisches Museum,
Vienna

Aphrodite

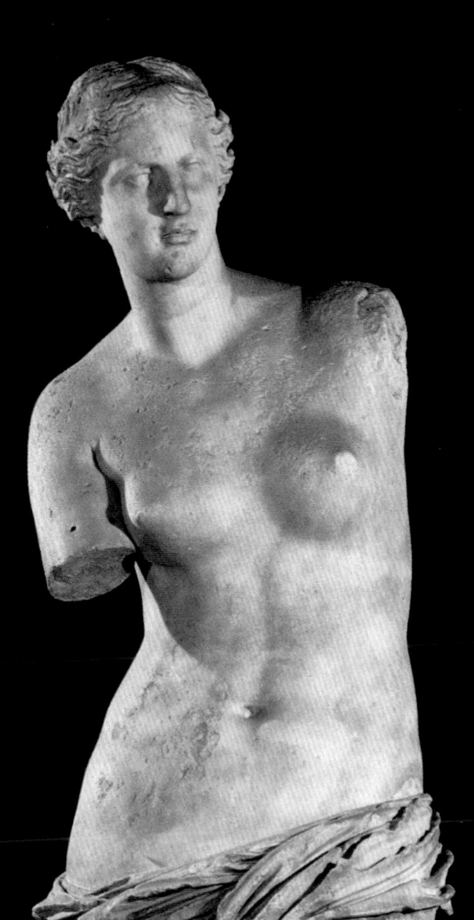

Among all the divinities on Mount Olympus, Aphrodite is by far the most celebrated in both ancient art and modern art. The goddess of beauty and of love, she was the object of cults all over the ancient world. The most famous festivals in her honor took place on the islands of Cythera and Cyprus, which according to myth were the places that welcomed her after her birth. The mother of Aeneas, the Trojan hero who founded Rome, Aphrodite was known to the Romans as Venus. The Roman emperor Julius Caesar built a temple dedicated to her, as she was considered the mother of the city, the Venus Genetrix. In this way, Rome claimed a remote divine origin for itself.

We have already told how, according to the narrative of Hesiod, Aphrodite rose from the foam (*aphros* in Greek) fertilized by the genitals of Uranus that were cut off by his son Cronus. This is the version of the goddess's birth that would become best known by artists and *The Birth of Venus* by Sandro Botticelli is one of the greatest examples. Another version of the birth of Aphrodite, going back to Homer, tells that she was a daughter of Zeus and Dione. The two traditions remained current throughout antiquity up until Plato, in his *Symposium*, imagined that there were actually two distinct Aphrodites: Aphrodite Ourania, or the "heavenly" Aphrodite, of whom Hesiod speaks in his *Theogony*, and Aphrodite Pandemos, or the "popular" Aphrodite, who dates back to the narrative of Homer. According to Pausanias, one of the speakers in the *Symposium*, the first Aphrodite is essentially spiritual, greater and more intelligent than the

Aphrodite
Attic cup
5th century BC

Ceramic
National
Archeological
Museum,
Florence

Venus
Copy from a Greek original by Praxiteles dated 350–340 BC
c. 100 BC

Marble
h. 82 ¼ in
(209 cm)
Musei Vaticani, Vatican City

second one, who is animated above all by a desire for physical satisfaction. Later, during the 15th century, the Neoplatonic poets and philosophers revived this duality and associated the idea of chaste love with the Heavenly Aphrodite (or Venus), while the Popular Aphrodite was connected to the idea of carnal love, tied to the senses, which was not considered sinful, but a passage by which one ascended to the other, higher sphere of love.

In Greek art from around the 5th century BC, Aphrodite is only depicted clothed, as we see on the Attic cup from the National Archeological Museum in Florence (see page 241). Later, the Athenian sculptor Praxiteles, who was active between 375 and 330 BC, established the type, or model, of a nude Aphrodite getting ready for the bath, which was taken up by other artists not only in the centuries that immediately followed, in the Greek and Roman worlds, but also in the Renaissance and in the neoclassic art of the 19th century. The sculpture of Praxiteles has not survived, but the model he created has come down to us through the many copies and variations it has inspired since the Hellenistic period. In the 1500s, identified by painters as the incarnation of beauty and sensuality, Aphrodite would sometimes take on the more worldly appearance of a courtesan, offering her nudity to the viewer in a moment of abandon and rest. This is the case with the *Sleeping Venus* by Giorgione (Dresden, Gemäldegalerie), which would furnish, moreover, the model for the many paintings of Venus by Titian, including the famous *Venus of Urbino* (Florence, Uffizi Gallery). Recalling

Sebastiano Ricci
Belluno, 1659–Venice, 1734

Venus and Cupid with Vulcan
c. 1697–1699

Oil on canvas
64 ¾ x 49 ¾ in
(164.5 x 126.5 cm)
Hermitage, St. Petersburg

244

the models furnished by these two painters of 16th century Venice, especially the *Venus of Urbino*, the painter Edouard Manet would in 1865 create his controversial *Olympia* (Paris, Musée d'Orsay)—a "modern" Venus, much more real and worldly—without subjecting the female nude to the traditional mythological or "historical" treatment that made nudity acceptable to the general public.

Aphrodite is not, however, a symbol only of beauty and love. Like the other gods on Olympus, she is personally involved in various actions. We have already spoken (see page 88) of her involvement in the abduction of Helen, which caused the Trojan war, and of her protection of Aeneas, and we will speak of her again in the chapters dedicated to that legendary war and the hero Aeneas. One of her rivals was Hera, the wife of Zeus, in whom Aphrodite often awakened a love for other women. But she was not satisfied with inciting love and passion in others. She herself took part in many amorous adventures. As Homer tells in the *Odyssey*, Aphrodite was married to Hephaestus, the god of fire and metallurgy, but she also took Ares, the god of war, as a lover. One morning, Helius, the sun god, surprised the two lovers together and told Hephaestus. Hurt by this, Hephaestus laid a trap, with a magic net that only he knew how to use. One night when the two lovers were lying together, Hephaestus covered them with the net and invited all the gods of Olympus to see the spectacle, which caused great hilarity. Ashamed, Aphrodite took refuge in Cypros and Ares in Thrace.

Cupid Bending his Bow

Roman copy of a Greek original by Lysippus of 335 BC (active 4th century BC)
1st century AD

Marble
47 ½ x 1 ¾ in
(121 cm x 4.5 cm)
Imperial Palace, Pavlovsk

This story about Aphrodite is a favorite with painters. Sometimes, she is depicted asleep next to Ares, as in the marvelous panel painting *Venus and Mars* from 1483 by Botticelli (London, National Gallery). This quiet scene, which gives no hint of the betrayal and revenge in Homer's narrative, presents itself as a Neoplatonic version of the myth, in which love has the power to placate violence. Other times, the painters show the moment that Hephaestus discovers the treachery, as in the painting *Venus, Vulcan, and Mars* from 1545–1550 by Jacopo Tintoretto (Munich, Alte Pinakothek).

Also linked to Aphrodite is the figure of Eros, the god of love. In Hesiod's *Theogony*, Eros comes directly out of the initial Chaos of the universe, like Gaia, the Earth, and Uranus, the Heavens. It is his job to maintain the internal cohesion of the cosmos and the continuity of the human race. In the myths that tell about the creation of the world and the appearance of the gods, Eros is an entity, or being, of fundamental importance. He does not, however, as would happen starting with the first generation of the gods, have a form, or shape. But there also exists another Eros, most often understood to be the result of the love affair between Aphrodite and Ares (other versions say that he is the son of Aphrodite and Hermes, or of Hermes and Artemis). This second type of Eros takes the form of a small child, most often with wings, armed with a bow and arrow. Wounding both gods and men with his weapon, he causes confusion in their hearts. And he is, therefore, both feared and respected. Eros often appears with

Luca Cambiaso
Moneglia, 1527–Madrid, 1585

Venus and Adonis
1583

Oil on canvas
55 ½ x 38 ½ in
(141 x 98 cm)
Galleria Borghese, Rome

Aphrodite, as in Botticelli's famous *Primavera* (Florence, Uffizi Gallery) and Correggio's *Education of Cupid* (London, National Gallery). There are many depictions of him together with Psyche and he often appears being punished for some misdeed, or absorbed in play, as in several frescoes from Pompeii.

Finally, we cannot close this brief study of Aphrodite without telling the sad story of Adonis, another subject that has been very popular in art. Mentioned by Apollodorus in his *Library* (III, 14), the story was most popular with the Romans, and it is in Ovid's *Metamorphoses* (X, 298–739) that we find the most detailed and well-known version. Seeking revenge, Aphrodite caused Myrrha to fall in love with her own father, Cinyras, who was king of Cyprus. Myrrha thus entered her father's bed, where she lay with him for several nights without revealing her identity. But Cinyras discovered that his lover was his own daughter. Pursued by her father, who wanted to kill her, the girl took refuge in the forest. Finally, in order to save her from an imminent nasty fate, the gods, who had been moved to pity, transformed her into a myrrh tree. The tree gave birth to a child, the fruit of an incestuous union, and it was named Adonis. Struck by his beauty and, according to Ovid, also by an arrow shot in error by Eros, Aphrodite took the child and entrusted him to Persephone (known to the Romans as Proserpina) to be raised. But even Persephone fell in love with him and did not want to give him back to Aphrodite. Zeus resolved the dispute by giving Adonis for one third of a year to Persephone, for one third to

Venus de Milo
From the island of Milos, Cyclades
c. 100 BC

Marble
h. 79 1/2 in
(202 cm)
Louvre,
Paris

Aphrodite, and for one third to whoever the boy should choose. Aphrodite tried to warn her beloved against the dangers of the hunt, but he would not listen to her and was killed by a boar sent by an angry Artemis.

Adonis appears in a 1st-century wall painting from Pompeii (Naples, National Archeological Museum) known as *The Wounded Adonis*. Beginning in the 16th century, he often appeared next to Aphrodite, in works that illustrated the various episodes of his brief life, starting with his birth from the trunk of a tree and ending with his death caused by a boar. Among the many artists who have depicted him are, in the 16th century, Titian, Paolo Veronese, and the Flemish painter Bartholomaeus Spranger; in the 17th century, Rubens, and Domenichino and Giovanni Battista Gaulli; and in the 18th century, the sculptor Giuseppe Mazzola.

The Birth of Venus

Relief from the Ludovisi Throne

460 BC

Marble
h. 38 ½ in (98 cm)
Palazzo Altemps, Rome

The Birth of Venus

1st century BC

Fresco
House of Venus in the Shell,
Pompeii

pp. 256–257

Sandro Botticelli

Florence, 1445–1510

The Birth of Venus

c. 1482

Tempera on canvas
72 ½ x 112 ½ in
(184.5 x 285.5 cm)
Uffizi Gallery, Florence

pp. 258–259

Alexandre Cabanel

Montpellier, 1823–Paris, 1889

The Birth of Venus

1863

Oil on canvas
51 x 88 ½ in
(130 x 225 cm)
Musée d'Orsay,
Paris

Odilon Redon

Bordeaux, 1840–Paris, 1916

The Birth of Venus

c. 1912

Pastel on paper
33 ¼ x 25 ½ in (84.4 x 65 cm)
Musée du Petit-Palais,
Paris

Medici Venus

Copy from a Greek original by Praxiteles
370–330 BC

Marble
h. 60 ¼ in (153 cm)
Uffizi Gallery,
Florence

Raphael (Raffaello Sanzio) and assistants
Urbino, 1483–Rome, 1520

Venus on a Chariot Pulled by Doves
c. 1518

Fresco
78 ³/₄ x 59 in
(200 x 150 cm)
Villa Farnesina, Loggia di Psyche, Rome

Giorgione (Giorgio da Castelfranco)

Castelfranco, Treviso, c. 1477–Venice, 1510

Sleeping Venus (Dresden Venus)

1509

Oil on canvas
42 ¾ x 68 ¾ in
(108.5 x 175 cm)
Gemäldegalerie Alte Meister, Dresden

266

pp. 268–269

Titian (Tiziano Vecellio)

Pieve di Cadore, Belluno, c. 1490–Venice, 1576

Venus of Urbino

1538

Oil on canvas
46 ¾ x 65 in
(119 x 165 cm)
Uffizi Gallery, Florence

Édouard Manet
Paris, 1832–1883

Olympia

1863

Oil on canvas
51 ¼ x 74 ¾ in
(130.5 x 190 cm)
Musée d'Orsay,
Paris

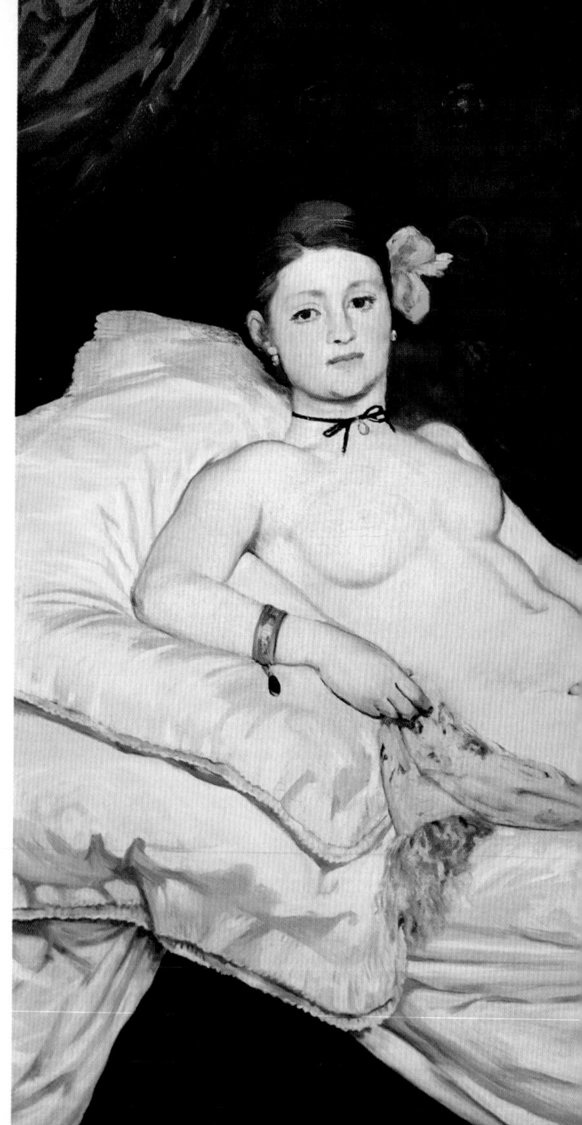

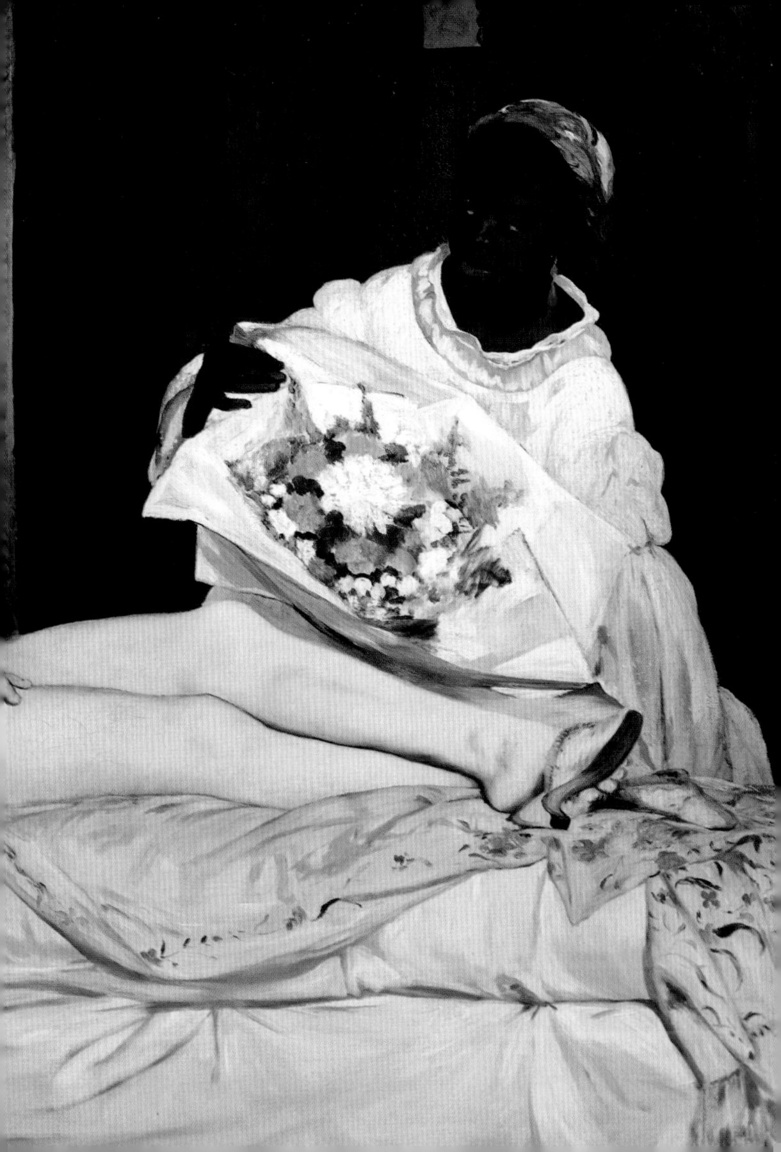

"AND WITH HER WENT EROS,
AND COMELY DESIRE FOLLOWED HER AT HER BIRTH AT THE FIRST
AND AS SHE WENT INTO THE ASSEMBLY OF THE GODS.
THIS HONOR SHE HAS FROM THE BEGINNING,
AND THIS IS THE PORTION ALLOTTED TO HER AMONGST MEN AND UNDYING GODS,
THE WHISPERINGS OF MAIDENS AND SMILES AND DECEITS
WITH SWEET DELIGHT AND LOVE AND GRACIOUSNESS."

(HESIOD, *THEOGONY*, 201-206)

Lucas Cranach the Elder
Kronach, 1472–Weimar, 1553

Venus and Cupid
1509

Oil on canvas
83 ¾ x 40 in (213 x 102 cm)
Hermitage,
St. Petersburg

PELLE · CVPIDINEOS · TOTO CONAMINE · LVXVS
NE · TVA · POSSIDEAT PECTORA · CECA · VENVS

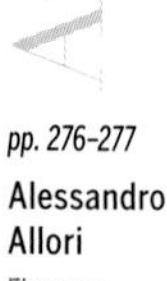

pp. 276-277

Alessandro Allori

Florence, 1535-1607

Venus and Cupid

c. 1569

Oil on canvas
51 x 84 ½ in (130 x 215 cm)
Musée des Beaux Arts, Auxerre

Lucas Cranach the Elder

Kronach, 1472-Weimar, 1553

Venus and Cupid

second version

1506

Print
10 ¾ x 7 ½ in (27.7 x 18.9 cm)
Kupferstich-Kabinett, Staatliche Kunstsammlungen, Dresden

L
1506
C

Tintoretto (Jacopo Robusti)
Venice, 1518–1594

Venus, Cupid, and Vulcan

c. 1550–1555

Oil on canvas
33 ½ x 77 ½ in (85 x 197 cm)
Palazzo Pitti, Galleria Palatina,
Florence

Venus and Mars

From the House of Mars and Venus, Pompeii

2nd century BC

Wall painting
National Archeological Museum, Naples

280

Aphrodite

Sandro Botticelli

Florence, 1445–1510

Venus and Mars

c. 1485

Tempera on panel
27 1/4 x 68 1/4 in (69.2 x 173.4 cm)
National Gallery,
London

pp. 284–285

Giulio Romano

Rome, c. 1499–Mantua, 1546

Venus and Mars Bathing

1526–1528

Fresco
Palazzo Tè, Sala di Amore e Psiche,
Mantua

Veronese (Paolo Caliari)

Verona, 1528–Venice, 1588

Mars and Venus with Cupid

c. 1577–1580

Oil on canvas
18 ½ x 18 ½ in (47 x47 cm)
Galleria Sabauda,
Turin

Tintoretto
(Jacopo Robusti)
Venice, 1518–1594

Mars and Venus Surprised by Vulcan

c. 1555

Oil on canvas
53 x 78 in
(135 x 198 cm)
Alte Pinakothek,
Munich

"AND VULCAN ... FROM LIQUID BRASS,
THOUGH SURE, YET SUBTLE SNARES
HE FORMS, AND NEXT A WOND'ROUS NET
PREPARES,
DRAWN WITH SUCH CURIOUS ART, SO
NICELY SLY,
UNSEEN THE MESHES CHEAT THE
SEARCHING EYE.
NOT HALF SO THIN THEIR WEBS THE
SPIDERS WEAVE,
WHICH THE MOST WARY, BUZZING PREY
DECEIVE.
THESE CHAINS, OBEDIENT TO THE TOUCH,
HE SPREAD
IN SECRET FOLDINGS OVER THE CONSCIOUS BED:
THE CONSCIOUS BED AGAIN WAS QUICKLY PREST
BY THE FOND PAIR, IN LAWLESS RAPTURES BLEST.
MARS WONDERED AT HIS CYTHEREA'S CHARMS,
MORE FAST THAN EVER LOCKED WITHIN HER
ARMS."

(OVID, *METAMORPHOSES*, IV)

Costantino Cedini
Padua, 1741–Venice, 1811

Mars and Venus Caught in Vulcan's Net

18th century

Fresco
Palazzo Emo Capodilista, Padua

"EROS, FAIREST AMONG THE DEATHLESS GODS,
WHO UNNERVES THE LIMBS
AND OVERCOMES THE MIND AND WISE
COUNSELS
OF ALL GODS AND ALL MEN WITHIN THEM."

(HESIOD, *THEOGONY*, 120-123)

Caravaggio (Michelangelo Merisi)

Caravaggio, Bergamo, 1571–Porto Ercole, Grosseto, 1610

Amor Victorious

c. 1602

Oil on canvas
61 ¼ x 44 ½ in (156 x 113 cm)
Staatliche Museen, Gemäldegalerie, Berlin

Jean-Antoine Watteau

Valenciennes, 1684–
Nogent-sur-Marne, 1721

Venus Disarming Cupid

c. 1715

Oil on canvas
18 ½ x 15 in (47 x 38 cm)
Musée Condé,
Chantilly

"AND OF A THOUSAND ARROWS CUPID CHOSE THE BEST:
NO FEATHER BETTER POISED, A SHARPER HEAD NONE HAD, AND SOONER NONE, AND SURER SPED."

(OVID, *METAMORPHOSES*, V, 379-382)

Carle Van Loo

Nice, 1705–Paris, 1765

Cupid Shooting a Bow

1761

Oil on canvas
46 ½ x 35 ½ in (118 x 90 cm)
Imperial Palace,
Pavlovsk

Paul Cézanne
Aix-en-Provence, 1839–1906

Still Life with Plaster Cupid
1894–1895

Oil on canvas
24 3/4 x 31 3/4 in
(63 x 81 cm)
Nationalmuseum, Stockholm

Jacques-Louis David

Paris, 1748–
Brussels, 1825

Sappho and Phaon

1809

Oil on canvas
88 ¾ x 103 in
(225.3 x 262 cm)
Hermitage,
St. Petersburg

Cupid and Psyche
From Pompeii
Terracotta

National Archeological Museum,
Naples

Cupid Kissing Psyche

From House VII, 2, 6, Pompeii

1st century AD

Wall painting
National Archeological Museum, Naples

Aphrodite

Raphael (Raffaello Sanzio) and assistants
Urbino, 1483–Rome, 1520

Cupid and the Three Graces
Scene from the cycle of Cupid and Psyche
c. 1518

Fresco
c. 79 x 59 in (200 x 150 cm)
Villa Farnesina, Loggia di Psyche, Rome

Workshop of Giulio Mazzoni and Daniele da Volterra

Psyche Uncovering the Sleeping Cupid

c. 1550

Fresco
Palazzo Spada-Capodiferro, Stanza di Psiche, Rome

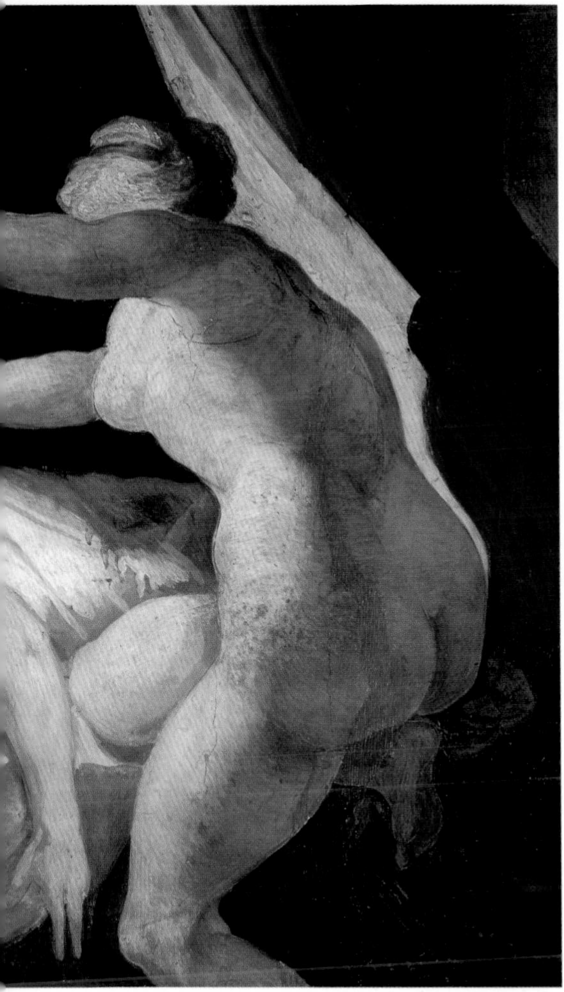

pp. 310-311

Giuseppe Maria Crespi (Lo Spagnolo)

Bologna, 1665-1747

Psyche Discovers Cupid

1707-1709

Oil on canvas
51 x 84 ½ in
(130 x 215 cm)
Uffizi Gallery, Florence

Perin del Vaga and assistants
Florence, 1501–Rome, 1547

Psyche Discovers Cupid and Cupid Flees
c. 1545–1546

Fresco
Castel Sant'Angelo, Stanza di Amore e Psiche, Rome

Anthony van Dyck

Antwerp, 1599–London, 1641

Cupid and Psyche

1639–1640

Oil on canvas
78 ¾ x 75 ¾ in
(200.2 x 192.6 cm)
Royal Collection of Her Majesty Queen Elizabeth II, Windsor Castle

Bénigne Gagnereaux
Dijon, 1756–
Florence, 1795

Psyche Roused by Cupid
c. 1780

Oil on canvas
Palazzo Altieri, Rome

Gaspare Landi
Piacenza, 1756–1830

Cupid and Psyche
After sculpture by Antonio Canova
c. 1787

Oil on canvas
37 3/4 x 38 1/2 in (96 x 98 cm)
Museo Correr,
Venice

Antonio Canova

Possagno, Treviso, 1757–Venice, 1822

Cupid and Psyche

1793

Marble
h. 61 in (155 cm)
Louvre,
Paris

"BUT WHEN SHE TOOK THE LAMP AND CAME
TO THE BED SIDE,
SHE SAW THE MOST MEEKE AND SWEETEST
BEAST OF ALL BEASTS,
EVEN FAIRE CUPID, COUCHED FAIRLY."

(APULEIUS, *METAMORPHOSES*, V, 22)

Johann Heinrich Füssli
Zurich, 1741–London, 1825

Cupid and Psyche

c. 1810

Oil on canvas
49 ¼ x 39 ¼ in (125 x 100 cm)
Kunsthaus,
Zurich

Giulio Romano

Rome, c. 1499–
Mantua, 1546

Mars Pursuing Adonis

1526–1528

Fresco
Palazzo Tè, Sala di Amore e Psiche, Mantua

Ferdinand Bol

Dordrecht, 1616–
Amsterdam, 1680

Venus and Adonis

c. 1657

Oil on canvas
66 x 90 ½ in
(168 x 230 cm)
Rijksmuseum,
Amsterdam

326

François Lemoyne

Paris, 1688-1737

Venus and Adonis

1729

Oil on canvas

36 ¼ x 28 ¾ in (92 x 73 cm)

Nationalmuseum,

Stockholm

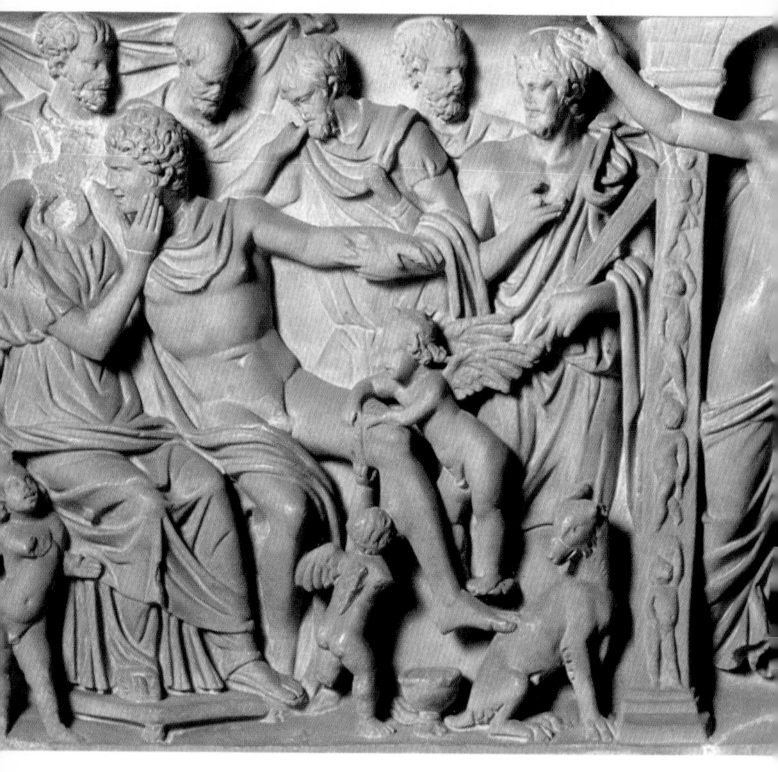

The Death of Adonis

Detail of a sarcophagus
2nd century

Marble
Palazzo Ducale, Mantua

pp. 332–333

Francesco Albani

Bologna, 1578–1660

The Death of Adonis

17th century

Oil on canvas
Musée des Beaux Arts,
Dunkerque

335

Sebastiano del Piombo

Venice, c. 1485–Rome, 1547

The Death of Adonis

c. 1512

Oil on canvas
74 ½ x 112 ½ in
(189 x 285.5 cm)
Uffizi Gallery,
Florence

"AND ADONIS, WHILE STILL A BOY,
WAS WOUNDED AND KILLED IN HUNTING
BY A BOAR
THROUGH THE ANGER OF ARTEMIS."

(APOLLODORUS, *LIBRARY*, III, 14, 4)

Giuseppe Mazzuoli
Siena, c. 1644–Rome, 1725

The Death of Adonis
1709

Marble
h. 76 in (193 cm)
Hermitage,
St. Petersburg

Jacopo Zanguidi (Il Bertoja)
Parma, 1544–Rome (?), c. 1573

Cupid Leading Venus to the Dying Adonis

c. 1560–1566

Oil on canvas
47 ¼ x 36 ¼ in (120 x 92 cm)
Louvre,
Paris

Nicolas Poussin

Les Andelys, 1594 –Rome, 1665

Venus Lamenting over Adonis

1625

Oil on canvas
22 ½ x 50 ¼ in
(57 x 128 cm)
Musée des Beaux Arts, Caen

340

Francesco Furini

Florence, 1603–1646

Venus Lamenting over Adonis

1628

Oil on canvas
91 ¾ x 74 ¾ in
(233 x 190 cm)
Szépmüvészeti Múzeum, Budapest

Apollo

Apollo Crowned with Laurel
Kylix
480–470 BC
Ceramic
Archeological Museum, Delphi

Apollo is another very important figure in Greek mythology and popular with artists. A son of Zeus and the twin brother of Artemis, Apollo belongs to the second generation of the Olympian gods. He is the god of light, beauty, and prophesy, as well as the inventor of music and the father of Asclepius, the god of medicine. Since antiquity, his iconographic attributes have been the lyre, the laurel, the bow, the arrow, and the quiver. In art since the Renaissance, the lyre, an ancient musical instrument, has sometimes been replaced by a lute or a viola di gamba. Apollo is sometimes accompanied by a raven or other bird that, as a bearer of omens, is a sign of his power of prophesy. And it is precisely with a raven and his crown of laurel and a lyre that we see him depicted on the inside of an Attic cup from the 5th century BC attributed to the painter of Eleusis (Delphi, Archeological Museum).

Apollo is also a warrior god, a characteristic that he shares with his twin sister Artemis. We see him involved in wars such as the Trojan war, in which he intervened on the side of the Trojans, and also in individual battles. Ordered by Zeus, Apollo went to Delphi, on Mount Parnassus, where a dragon was on a rampage in the city. The Python—as the monster was known—plundered the countryside, muddied the waters of streams and springs, wiped out herds, and killed the peasants. Apollo killed the monster with his arrows and liberated Delphi from this scourge. For this reason, he was called Pythian Apollo. In this way, he became master of the oracle of the sanctuary at Delphi, which had been dedicated to Themis—one of the Titans, the goddess of justice, and also one of the divine wives of Zeus. The

Abraham Jamnitzer

"Daphne" drinking vessel

Late 16th century

Silver, gold plate, coral
Staatliche Kunstsammlungen, Dresden

sanctuary became the primary location in the Greek world for the cult of Apollo. Kings, heroes, and common citizens all went there in order to hear the oracle uttered by the priestess who lived inside the temple, and who was known as the Pythia. Dedicated to the cult of Apollo, the Athenians, Thebans, Syracusans, Corinthians, and many others paid homage to the god and placed treasures inside the sanctuary, which housed various kinds of votive and commemorative statues. Despite the fact that it has come down to us in a state of ruin caused by various earthquakes and fires, and by being abandoned after the rise of Christianity, today it is still possible to understand the importance that the sanctuary of Apollo at Delphi had for the ancient world when one approaches the temple on what is now known as the Via Sacra, along which were displayed numerous treasures and hundreds of art works from all over Greece and the Hellenic world.

Although it was of fundamental importance for the establishment of the cult of Apollo, the killing of the Python was not the episode most favored by artists. Starting in the 1400s, by far the most popular with artists were the stories of his musical contests with Marsyas (or Pan) and, above all, those of his sorrowful love for Daphne. According to the version by Ovid (*Metamorphoses*, I, 452–477), Daphne was the daughter of the river Peneus, which flowed in Thessaly (although another version says that her parents were Gaia, the Earth, and the river Ladon). Angry with Apollo, who had mocked him while he practiced with his bow and arrow, Eros caused him to fall in love with Daphne, at the same time taking care to make her

Luca Giordano
Naples, 1634–1705

Apollo Flaying Marsyas
1678

Oil on canvas
88 ½ x 63 in
(225 x 160 cm)
Museo Bardini, Florence

feel a desire to reject him. This was accomplished by wounding Apollo with a golden arrow, which aroused feelings of love, and by wounding Daphne with an arrow of lead, which caused feelings of love to vanish. Apollo pursued Daphne and, when she realized that she could not escape him, Daphne prayed to her father for help. Peneus then transformed her into a laurel (*dafne*, in Greek), a tree that then became sacred to Apollo.

This particular legend was the figurative theme for one of the first paintings of a mythological subject after the long absence of myth from art caused by the rise of Christianity. It was the *Apollo and Daphne* from around 1475 by the Florentine painter Antonio del Pollaiolo (London, National Gallery) and it shows Apollo putting his arms around Daphne at the precise moment she begins her transformation. Apollo's dismayed look is answered by the victorious smile of Daphne. The 15th-century clothing worn by Apollo and Daphne—clearly not worn in ancient times—reminds us that the subject of the painting is in accord with the Neoplatonic interpretation of the myth and compatible with Christian morality, which sees in chastity a virtue that is superior to sensual love. Another spectacular depiction of the myth is the sculptural group *Apollo and Daphne* from 1622–1625 by Gian Lorenzo Bernini (Rome, Galleria Borghese).

Among depictions of the musical competition between Apollo and the satyr Marsyas are the paintings *Apollo and Marsyas* by Pietro Perugino (Paris, Louvre), *The Flaying of Marsyas* by Titian (Kromeriz, Archbishop's Palace), and *Apollo and Marsyas* by Luca Giordano (Naples, Museo Capodimonte).

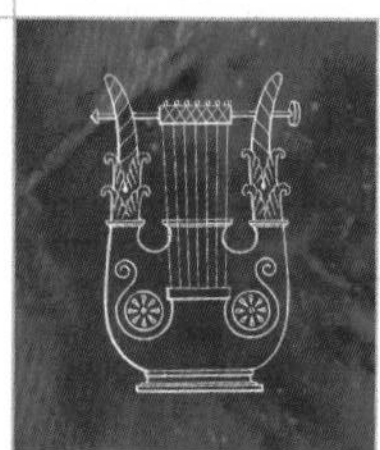

Apollo Belvedere

Roman copy of a Greek original in bronze
c. 330-320 BC,
with integrations of the 16th century
130–140 AD

Marble
h. 88 in (224 cm)
Museo Pio-Clementino,
Giardino del Belvedere,
Vatican City

Apollo Citharist

c. 30 BC

Fresco
22 x 27 in
(56 x 69 cm)
Museo Palatino,
Antiquarium
Palatino,
Rome

pp. 356–357

Apollo Slaying the Python
Detail
c. 65–70 AD

Fresco in IVth style
Triclinium, House of Vettii,
Pompeii

Diego
Velázquez
Seville, 1599–
Madrid, 1660

The Forge of Vulcan

1629

Oil on canvas
87 ³/₄ x 114 in
(223 x 290 cm)
Prado,
Madrid

pp. 358–359

Marten de Vos
Antwerp,
c. 1532–1603

Apollo and the Muses

1580

Oil on panel
17 ³/₄ x 25 in
(45 x 64 cm)
Musées Royaux
des Beaux-Arts,
Brussels

François Girardon

Troyes, 1628–
Paris, 1715

Thomas Regnaudin

Moulins, 1622–
Paris, 1706

Apollo Attended by the Nymphs of Thetis

1666–1675

Marble
Castle Park,
Versailles

Andrea Appiani
Milan, 1754–1817

The Chariot of Apollo

1800–1810

Charcoal on carton
56 ½ x 90 ½ in
(oval)
(144 x 230 cm)
Pinacoteca
di Brera,
Milan

pp. 364–365

Giovanni
Battista Tiepolo
Venice, 1696–
Madrid, 1770

The Four Continents

detail showing the chariot of Apollo

1750–1753

Fresco
Residenz
Würzburg,
Würzburg

"SUCH WAS THE GOD, AND SUCH THE FLYING FAIR,
SHE URGED BY FEAR, HER FEET DID SWIFTLY MOVE,
BUT HE MORE SWIFTLY, WHO WAS URGED BY LOVE.
HE GATHERS GROUND UPON HER IN THE CHASE;
NOW BREATHES UPON HER HAIR, WITH NEARER PACE
AND JUST IS FASTENING ON THE WISHED EMBRACE.
THE NYMPH GREW PALE, AND IN A MORTAL FRIGHT,
SPENT WITH THE LABOR OF SO LONG A FLIGHT;
AND NOW DESPAIRING, CAST A MOURNFUL LOOK
UPON THE STREAMS OF HER PATERNAL BROOK;
'OH HELP', SHE CRYED, 'IN THIS EXTREMEST NEED!
IF WATER GODS ARE DEITIES INDEED:
GAPE EARTH, AND THIS UNHAPPY WRETCH INTOMB;
OR CHANGE MY FORM, WHENCE ALL MY SORROWS COME'.
SCARCE HAD SHE FINISHED, WHEN HER FEET SHE FOUND
BENUMBED WITH COLD, AND FASTENED TO THE GROUND;
A FILMY RIND ABOUT HER BODY GROWS.
HER HAIR TO LEAVES, HER ARMS EXTEND TO BOUGHS:
THE NYMPH IS ALL INTO A LAWREL GONE;
THE SMOOTHNESS OF HER SKIN REMAINS ALONE."

(OVID, *METAMORPHOSES*, I)

Antonio del Pollaiolo
Florence, c. 1432–Rome, 1498

Apollo and Daphne
c. 1470–1480

Tempera on panel
11 1/2 x 7 3/4 in
(29.5 x 20 cm)
National Gallery, London

Gian Lorenzo Bernini

Naples, 1598–Rome, 1680

Apollo and Daphne

1622–1625

Marble
95 ½ in (243 cm)
Borghese Gallery,
Rome

Daphne Transformed into Laurel

Plate in majolica based on a drawing by C. Delange and C. Borneman

1869

Edition Delange, Paris

Pietro Perugino

Città della Pieve, 1445/50-Fontignano, Perugia, 1523

Apollo and Marsyas

c. 1495-1500

Oil on canvas
15 ¼ x 11 ¼ in (39 x 29 cm)
Louvre,
Paris

Titian (Tiziano Vecellio)

Pieve di Cadore, Belluno, c. 1490–Venice, 1576

The Flaying of Marsyas

1570

Oil on canvas
83 ½ x 81 ½ in
(212 x 207 cm)
Archiepiscopal Gallery, Kromeriz

Jusepe Ribera (Lo Spagnoletto)
Játiva, 1591–Naples, 1652

The Flaying of Marsyas
1637

Oil on canvas
71 ½ x 91 ¼ in
(182 x 232 cm)
Museo Nazionale di Capodimonte, Naples

pp. 380–381

Montalto

Treviglio, Bergamo, 1612–Milan, 1690

Apollo Flaying Marsyas

c. 1677–1682

Oil on canvas
57 ¾ x 81 in
(147 x 206 cm)
Castello Sforzesco, Museo d'Arte Antica, Milan

Giovanni Battista Tiepolo

Venice, 1696–Madrid, 1770

The Death of Hyacinth

1752–1753

Oil on canvas
113 x 92 ½ in
(287 x 235 cm)
Museo Thyssen-Bornemisza, Madrid

Athena

The giant gold and ivory statue of Athena (40 feet/12 meters tall) by the great 5th-century BC Greek sculptor Phidias, known through copies, including the Roman one called *Athena the Beautiful*, reminds us that this incredible goddess, capable of standing up to her father, Zeus, and the symbol of wisdom, was also the patron god of the city of Athens, which takes its name from her. The very astute goddess fought at her father's side in the battle against the Giants and managed to put the terrible Enceladus out of action by hurling the entire island of Sicily at him. Although a war goddess, she was more of a strategist than warlike. Odysseus (Ulysses) was among the heroes she protected and the goddess helped him to overcome all the obstacles encountered in his long and difficult journey back to Ithaca after the Trojan war. Athena opposed the passions of love and instinct with reason and decided to remain a virgin.

The oldest literary sources all give more or less the same version of the goddess's spectacular birth. According to Hesiod in the *Theogony* (886–900), after getting rid of his father, Zeus first wed Metis, daughter of the Titan Oceanus and the Titanide Tethys. When Metis became pregnant, Uranus and Gaia warned the king of the gods that while the firstborn would be a girl, as strong and intelligent as her father, a second male child would be born to Metis who would deprive Zeus of his kingdom. The alarmed god, like Cronus with his children before him, swallowed his pregnant wife. According to the Homeric Hymns (*Hymn to Athena,* 27), Athena burst forth from her father's head in full armor and

Minerva

2nd century BC

Marble
h. 126 ¼ in
(321 cm)
Musei Capitolini,
Atrio del Palazzo
Nuovo,
Rome

Athena
Amphora
5th century BC

Ceramic
Ashmolean
Museum,
Oxford

as soon as she saw the light uttered a cry so loud that it made the earth tremble and raised waves at sea. Her potent cry is also mentioned in Pindar's verses dedicated to the goddess (*Olympians*, VII, 36). Then, to everyone's relief, the goddess lay down her arms. In his *Library* (1,3), Apollodorus adds that when the baby was about to be born, Zeus ordered Prometheus to break his head open with an axe and also alludes to a variation on the myth according to which it was Hephaestus (Vulcan) who wielded the axe.

In another episode, the goddess was involved in a dispute with Poseidon (Neptune) over who would be the patron god of Athens. It was decided that each of the contenders should make a gift to the city. A jury composed of the other gods of Olympus would decide which was the greatest gift. Poseidon thrust his trident into the rock on the Acropolis and water came forth. For her part, Athena stamped her foot on the ground and the first olive tree grew in the imprint. The gods decided in Athena's favor. For this reason the city was named Athens and, in her honor, the Parthenon—the largest temple in the ancient world— was built on the Acropolis and contained the aforementioned statue of the goddess by Phidias. The word *parthenos* in Greek means "virgin."

The cult of Athena was not limited to Athens. Other temples dedicated to her were built at Sparta, Megara, and Argos. There was even a temple dedicated to her near the Sanctuary of Apollo, at Delphi, known as the Sanctuary of Athena Pronaia. Although much smaller than the one dedicated to

Athena
Roman copy from the original by Cephisodotus
4th century BC
1st–2nd century AD
Marble
h. 55 in (140 cm)
Louvre,
Paris

the god of sun and music, Athena's sanctuary was meant to offer protection to Apollo. In Greek, the word *pronaia* means "she who stands in front."

A legend told by Ovid in his *Metamorphoses* (VI, 5–145), sees Athena involved in another competition, this time with a mortal. In this case it was Arachne, a young woman from Lydia, who was greatly talented in the arts of weaving and embroidery. This earned her the admiration of the Nymphs who came to watch her work. But the young woman refused to attribute her gift to Athena (Minerva, in Ovid's account), the goddess of ingenuity and crafts, and patroness of spinners, weavers, and embroiderers. She even challenged the goddess. At first Athena appeared to Arachne as an old woman and tried to convince her to apologize to the goddess but Arachne merely insulted her and asked why the goddess did not come herself. So Athena revealed her true identity and the competition began. Athena wove a tapestry depicting her competition with Poseidon for the city of Athens, in which the other gods of Olympus also appeared. The petulant Arachne depicted the least creditable love affairs of the gods, with their deceitful seductions and kidnappings. In anger over the young woman's work—which was perfect—Athena struck Arachne several times with a shuttle. Arachne tried to hang herself but Athena, moved to pity, would not let her die and turned her into a spider. And so, even today, Arachne continues to spin and weave (the Greek word *arachne* means spider).

Athena with Helmet and Shield
Detail of a greave from the Gladiators Barracks, Pompeii
14–69 AD

Bronze
National Archeological Museum, Naples

The transformation of the many episodes of Athena's life into images range from the classical raffigurations of her birth, fully armed, from Zeus's head, to the Neoplatonic Renaissance moral and allegorical works, such as the *Triumph of Virtue* by Andrea Mantegna, or *Pallas and the Centaur* by Botticelli, in which the goddess is shown, respectively, as she fights evil and while she tames the irrational and vicious Centaur. In this last scene, the olive branches that crown the goddess and wrap themselves around her arms and breast are a reminder of her dispute with Poseidon for the dominion of Athens when the goddess gifted the tree to the city. Sometimes, the head of the gorgon Medusa, who turned anyone who looked in her eyes to stone, is shown on the goddess' shield or aegis. According to the myth, Perseus gave this to her after beheading the monster. Thus, without having to fight, Athena could turn her enemies to stone. In this sense, Caravaggio's painting (Florence, Uffizi Gallery) in the form of a shield showing the *Head of Medusa* can be interpreted as a depiction of Athena's shield.

"AND AWE SEIZED ALL THE GODS AS THEY GAZED:
ATHENA SPRANG QUICKLY FROM THE IMMORTAL HEAD
AND STOOD BEFORE ZEUS WHO HOLDS THE AEGIS,
SHAKING A SHARP SPEAR..."

(*HOMERIC HYMNS*, XXVIII, "HYMN TO ATHENA," 6-9)

The Birth of Athena

Attic amphora

6th century BC

Ceramic

h. 15 3/4 in (h. 40.1 cm)

Louvre,

Paris

“PALLAS ATHENA, THE GLORIOUS GODDESS, BRIGHT-EYED, INVENTIVE,
UNBENDING OF HEART, PURE VIRGIN, SAVIOR OF CITIES, COURAGEOUS...”

(*HOMERIC HYMNS*, XXVIII,
“HYMN TO ATHENA,” 1-3)

pp. 396–397

Paolo Fiammingo
Antwerp, 1540–1596

The Birth of Athena
1590

Oil on canvas
41 ¾ x 60 ¼ in (106 x 153 cm)
Gallery of the Castle, Prague

Sandro Botticelli
Florence, 1445–1510

Pallas and the Centaur
c. 1482

Tempera on canvas
81 ½ x 58 ¼ in (207 x 148 cm)
Uffizi Gallery, Florence

Andrea Mantegna

Isola di Carturo, Padua, 1431–Mantua, 1506

The Triumph of Virtue

1502

Oil on canvas
63 x 75 ½ in
(160 x 192 cm)
Louvre,
Paris

Tintoretto (Jacopo Robusti)
Venice, 1518–1594

Pallas Dismissing Mars
1576

Oil on canvas
58 ¼ x 66 in
(148 x 168 cm)
Palazzo Ducale,
Venice

402

Lavinia Fontana

Bologna, 1552–Rome, 1614

Minerva Dressing

1613

Oil on canvas
101 ½ x 74 ¾ in (258 x 190 cm)
Galleria Borghese,
Rome

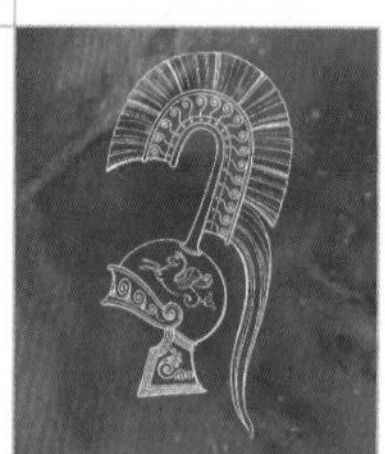

Rembrandt Harmenszoon van Rijn

Leiden, 1606–Amsterdam, 1669

Pallas Athena

1664–1665

Oil on canvas
46 ½ x 35 ¾ in (118 x 91 cm)
Museu Gulbenkian,
Lisbon

Athena and Poseidon

1st century BC

Cameo in sardonic agate
2 x 1 ½ in
(5.1 x 4.2 cm)
National Archeological Museum, Farnese Collection, Naples

pp. 412–413

Tintoretto (Jacopo Robusti)
Venice, 1518–1594

Athena and Arachne

c. 1579

Oil on canvas
47 x 107 in
(145 x 272 cm)
Uffizi Gallery, Florence

Domenico Pozzi
Castello S. Pietro, Canton Ticino, 1744–Milan, 1796

Competition between Poseidon and Minerva for the Patronage of the City of Athens

1789

Fresco
Villa Olmo, Como

pp. 414-415

Diego Velázquez
Seville, 1599–
Madrid, 1660

The Fable of Arachne (Las Hilanderas)

c. 1659

Oil on canvas
86 ½ x 113 ¾ in
(220 x 289 cm)
Prado,
Madrid

Athena and Perseus with the Gorgon

Fragment of a clay slab

44 BC–14 AD

Terracotta
with traces of
polychromy
29 x 23 ½ in
(74 x 60 cm)
Museo Palatino,
Rome

Caravaggio (Michelangelo Merisi)

Caravaggio, Bergamo, 1571–
Porto Ercole, Grosseto, 1610

Medusa

c. 1597

Oil on canvas sized on panel
diam. c. 21 ½ in (55 cm)
Uffizi Gallery,
Florence

Minor Gods

The "minor" gods are those who do not have their own seat on Mount Olympus, such as Hades (known to the Romans as Pluto), Persephone (Proserpina), Dionysus (Bacchus), Eros (Amore), Helios (Sole), and Pan, as well as those who are the children of a god and a mortal, such as Asclepius (Aesculapius). The fact of being "minor" does not mean that less attention has been paid to them by artists. On the contrary, Dionysus is by far one of the most popular mythological subjects. In this chapter, with the exception of Dionysus, who has a separate chapter devoted to him, we will discuss the myths concerning some of these gods and their treatment in the history of art.

We begin with Hades, the brother of Zeus and Poseidon. In the war against the Titans, during which Hades was allied with Zeus, the Cyclopes gave him a helmet that made the wearer invisible—which was the meaning of his name, *Haides*, in Greek. After the defeat of the Titans, he was made ruler of the regions below the earth—that is, Tartarus, or the Underworld (Hell). Hades was, therefore, the master of the Underworld and for this reason he did not participate in matters that involved life on the earth or on the seas, which were the prerogative of Zeus and Poseidon. In his own kingdom, however, he was implacable. Whoever entered there and consumed food was not permitted to leave. His helpers were Charon, who ferried the souls of the dead on their way to Tartarus across the river Acheron, and the terrible Cerberus, a three-headed dog that guarded the entrance to Hell.

Demeter and Persephone
Greek amphora
Late 7th century BC
Ceramic
h. 12 ¼ in (31.1 cm)
Szépművészeti Múzeum, Budapest

Gian Lorenzo Bernini
Naples, 1598–Rome, 1680

Pluto and Proserpina
1621–1622

Marble
100 ¼ in (255 cm)
Galleria Borghese, Rome

The legends refer to Hades constantly—and, when using his name, ancient authors often referred to the Underworld region itself—, but as a figure he usually remains in the background. Nevertheless, one particular episode has him as its protagonist and involves his sister Demeter (known to the Romans as Ceres) and her daughter, Persephone. Demeter, the goddess of the fertility of the earth and one of the divinities on Mount Olympus, gave birth to Persephone (known to the Romans as Proserpina) as the result of her union with her brother Zeus. According to the account in the *Homeric Hymn to Demeter*, the young girl was leading a carefree life among the nymphs when her uncle Hades, with the help of that same Zeus, carried her off. While Persephone was gathering flowers in a meadow, Zeus caused her to see a daffodil that was irresistably beautiful and fragrant. When the girl bent forward to pick it, the earth opened beneath her feet. Out came Hades in a golden chariot drawn by two horses. He seized her and carried her off with him to his underworld kingdom. When Demeter became aware of the absence of her daughter, she searched for her desperately all over the world, torch in hand. Helios, the sun god, who sees everything, told her what had happened. But that was not enough to bring back her daughter. Because of Demeter's deep sadness, the earth became sterile and the human race would have died of starvation if Zeus, moved to pity, had not commanded Hades to restore the girl to the world of the living. But she had already eaten the kernel of a pomegranate given to her by Hades, and therefore could not leave. So, finding a

Pan
1st century BC
Terracotta
h. 3 ½ (9 cm)
from Gerasa (Jerash), Jordan

compromise that would satisfy everyone, Zeus ordered that Persephone spend two-thirds of each year with her mother and the other gods of Mount Olympus, and one-third with Hades in his underground kingdom of darkness. The eight months spent in the world of the living correspond to the seasons when the plant world flourishes, when Demeter is happy and carries out her duties as the goddess of fertility. The other four months, obviously, correspond to winter, the season in which the earth is unproductive.

In ancient times and since the Renaissance, whenever mythological subjects are represented, Hades is depicted above all in the episode of the abduction of Persephone. An Apulian red-figure krater from the 4th century BC (London, British Museum) shows him leading her to the Underworld. One of the most intense representations in the modern era is the sculptural group *Pluto and Proserpina* from 1621–22 by Gian Lorenzo Bernini (Rome, Galleria Borghese), along with the painting *The Abduction of Proserpina* from 1631 by Rembrandt (Berlin, Gemäldegalerie).

The figure of Pan, the god of shepherds, of woodlands, and of flocks, also appears often in art. In this case as well, the primary source—or at least the oldest one—for the myth is a Homeric hymn, the *Hymn to Pan*, to which we refer below. It is also mentioned by, among others, Ovid (*Fasti*, II, 267), Apollodorus (*Library*, I, 13), and Plutarch (*On the Decline of the Oracles*, 419, b-d). Born from the union of Hermes with the daughter of Dryops, a descendent of Apollo and

Sèvres Manufacture

Pan
Detail of a vase
c. 1813

Porcelain
22 ¾ x 13 ¼ in
(58 x 34 cm)
Private collection,

part of the group that was believed to be among the first inhabitants of the Greek peninsula, Pan was rejected by his mother because of his demoniacal appearance: his lower limbs were those of a goat, he had two horns on his forehead and a prominent chin covered by a beard. His expression was both shrewd and beastly. Hermes carried him away to Mount Olympus, where the other gods, cheered by his presence, called him Pan (from his name in Greek which means "all" or "everything"), because he was welcome to all the gods. But this is not the only version of his origin. For the Romans, Pan was identified with Faunus. He lived in the woods and stayed close to springs, where he sought cool water. He did not like to be disturbed when he was resting. He embodied sexual desire and, in order to satisfy it, pursued both nymphs and boys. He was, in effect, a synthesis of the animal instinct and pastoral life.

Pan was thought to be the inventor of the syrinx, a flute made from reeds of various lengths and known as "the flute of Pan." It was named after Syrinx, a nymph of Arcadia who ran into a river in order to escape Pan and was turned into a reed. As a musician, Pan sometimes took the place of Marsyas in the legend about the musical contest with Apollo. In that version, told by Ovid (*Metamorphoses*, XI, 146–194), Pan does not meet the same nasty end as Marsyas, who is flayed by Apollo. The one who did pay a price was Midas, the king of Phrygia, who, acting as a judge in the competition on Mount Tmolus, chose Pan as the winner over Apollo. As a result, Apollo caused him to sprout the ears of an ass on his head.

Pan
c. 1665
Marble
Giardino
Buonaccorsi,
Potenza Picena

Very popular with artists since ancient times, Pan is often represented in the festive and happy processions led by Dionysus. But it was not unusual to see him play his flute in the company of nymphs, as in the fragment of an ancient relief *Pan Plays While Three Nymphs Dance* (Athens, National Archaeological Museum) and in the 1st-century fresco from Pompeii known as *Pan and the Nymphs* (Naples, National Archeological Museum). A painting by Jacob Jordaens titled *Pan and Syrinx* from around 1625 (Antwerp, Musée Royal des Beaux-Arts) reminds us of the amorous feats of the shepherd god.

Among the minor gods, we again mention Asclepius, a hero and the god of medicine. There are two versions of his birth. According to one, he is the result of the love between Apollo and Coronis, the daughter of Phlegyas, the king of Thessaly (*Homeric Hymn to Asclepius*; Pindar, *Pythian Odes*, 3; and Ovid, *Metamorphoses*, II, 535). According to another, he is the son of Apollo by Arsinoe, one of the daughters of Leucippus, a descendent of Perseus and the ruler of Messenia (although this is the version mentioned by Apollodorus in his *Library*, III, 10, Apollodorus also mentions the other one). Apollo entrusted the boy to the centaur Chiron, the tutor of, among others, heroes such as Achilles and Jason. From Chiron, Asclepius learned the art of medicine and became so skilled that he was even able to revive the dead. The sources mention many people brought back to life by him, including Hippolytus, the son of Theseus,

Apollonian Gods

From Pompeii

90–20 BC

Fresco in 2nd style
National Archeological Museum, Naples

Pluto Leading Persephone to the Underworld
Red-figure Apulian krater
360–350 BC

Ceramic
h. c. 8 ½ in
(22 cm)
British Museum,
London

who loved the hunt and was devoted to Artemis. In the eyes of Zeus these resurrections were a violation of the natural order of the world, and he hurled a thunderbold at Asclepius, killing him. This aroused the anger of Apollo, who, to avenge himself, killed the Cyclopes. What then followed is told by Euripides in the prologue to his tragedy *Alcestis.* In order to punish Apollo, Zeus forced him to work for one year in the service of a mortal, Admetus, the lord of Pherae in Thessaly, whose wife was Alcestis, and Apollo tended his herds. The figure of Asclepius is, at first, a hero. Nevertheless, the cult dedicated to him in the sanctuary at Epidaurus, as well as others, established him as a god.

Asclepius is usually shown with a staff around which a serpent is twisted. He is seen this way in ancient sculpture and again in the Renaissance. A wall painting from the first century (Naples, National Archaeological Museum) shows him with the centaur Chiron and his divine father, Apollo.

Agostino Carracci

Bologna, 1557–
Parma, 1602

Pluto in Repose with Cerberus and Triton

c. 1592–1593

Oil on canvas
43 x 21 in
(109 x 130 cm)
Galleria Estense,
Modena

Rembrandt Harmenszoon van Rijn
Leiden, 1606–Amsterdam, 1669

The Abduction of Proserpina
1631

Oil on panel
33 x 31 ¼ in
(84.8 x 79.7 cm)
Staatliche Museen, Gemäldegalerie, Berlin

Dante Gabriel Rossetti
London, 1828–Birchington-on-Sea, 1882

Proserpina
Study
1871

Pastel
38 ¼ x 18 ¼ in (97.1 x 46.3 cm)
Ashmolean Museum,
Oxford

Three Nymphs, Hermes, and Pan

Detail of the reliefs from the Caves of Pentele

4th century BC

Marble
h. 27 ½ in (70 cm)
National Archeological Museum, Athens

"MUSE, TELL ME ABOUT PAN, THE DEAR SON
OF HERMES,
WITH HIS GOAT'S FEET AND TWO HORNS,
A LOVER OF MERRY NOISE.
THROUGH WOODED GLADES HE WANDERS
WITH DANCING NYMPHS
WHO FOOT IT ON SOME SHEER CLIFF'S EDGE,
CALLING UPON PAN, THE SHEPHERD-GOD,
LONG-HAIRED, UNKEMPT.
HE HAS EVERY SNOWY CREST AND THE
MOUNTAIN PEAKS
AND ROCKY CRESTS FOR HIS DOMAIN."

(*HOMERIC HYMNS*, XIX, "HYMN TO PAN," 1-7)

Pan and the Maenads
Detail from an Italiot krater
4th century BC

Ceramic
Eolian Museum,
Lipari

Dionysiac Frieze
Detail
79 AD

Fresco
h. 63 ¾ in (162 cm)
Villa dei Misteri, Sala del Grande Dipinto,
Pompeii

Peter Paul Rubens

Siegen, 1577–
Antwerp, 1640

Jan Bruegel the Elder

Brussels, 1568–
Antwerp, 1625

Pan and Syrinx

c. 1617

Oil on panel
15 ¾ x 24 in
(40.3 x 61 cm)
Staatliche Museen
Kassel

Alessandro Turchi (l'Orbetto)

Verona, c. 1578–Rome, c. 1650

Pan and Syrinx

1620

Oil on canvas
48 x 58 ¼ in
(122 x 148 cm)
Imperial Palace, Pavlosk

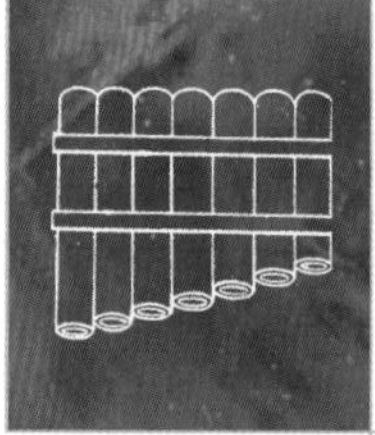

Nicolas Poussin

Les Andelys, 1594–Rome, 1665

Pan and Syrinx

1637

Oil on canvas
41 ¾ x 32 ¼ in (106 x 82 cm)
Gemäldegalerie Alte Meister,
Dresden

Jacob Jordaens

Antwerp, 1593-1678

Pan (Satyr Playing the Flute)

c. 1625

Oil on canvas
53 x 69 ¼ in
(135 x 176 cm)
Rijksmuseum,
Amsterdam

Arnold Böcklin

Basel, 1827–
San Domenico,
Florence, 1901

Idyll (Pan between Columns)

1875

Oil on canvas
24 ½ x 19 ¾ in
(62.7 x 50.2 cm)
Neue Pinakothek,
Munich

Minor Gods

pp. 460–461

Jacob Jordaens
Antwerp, 1593–1678

Apollo Defeating Pan
1637

Oil on canvas
71 ¼ x 105 in
(181 x 267 cm)
Prado,
Madrid

"MIDAS ALONE DISSATISFYED APPEARED:
TO HIM UNJUSTLY GIVEN THE JUDGMENT SEEMS,
FOR PAN'S BARBARICK NOTES HE MOST ESTEEMS.
THE LYRICK GOD, WHO THOUGHT HIS UNTUNED EAR
DESERVED BUT ILL A HUMAN FORM TO WEAR,
OF THAT DEPRIVES HIM, AND SUPPLIES THE PLACE
WITH SOME MORE FIT, AND OF AN AMPLER SPACE:
FIXED ON HIS NODDLE AN UNSEEMLY PAIR,
FLAGGING, AND LARGE, AND FULL OF WHITISH HAIR."

(OVID, *METAMORPHOSES*, XI)

Domenichino (Domenico Zampieri) and assistants
Bologna, 1581–Naples, 1641

The Judgement of Midas
1616–1618

Fresco transferred to canvas and sized on panel
105 x 88 in (267 x 224 cm)
National Gallery,
London

Dionysus

Guido Reni
Bologna, 1575–1642

Drinking Bacchus
1637–38

Oil on canvas
28 ¼ x 22 in
(72 x 56 cm)
Gemäldegalerie
Alte Meister,
Dresden

Dionysus, who was known to the Romans as Bacchus, is one of the most popular gods from classical mythology in the history of art. The god of wine and of plant life, he is associated with festivals, with dance, and with excess—that is, with everything that takes man outside of his daily routine. The son of Zeus and Semele, he suffered the persecution of Hera. On his various journeys fleeing her wrath, Dionysus established vineyards and thus became the god of wine. His story is linked to that of Ariadne, who, abandoned by Theseus, was rescued by the god and became his wife (see page 656). He is often seen on antique reliefs and painted vases, depicted with a crown of ivy or vine leaves and surrounded by nymphs, sileni, satyrs, and maenads. Dionysus was a favorite of sculptors and painters in the Renaissance, the baroque era, and afterwards. Michelangelo, Bellini, Titian, Carracci, Caravaggio, Reni, and Poussin are just a few of the artists who have dedicated works to him.

The story of the birth of Dionysus is one of the most dramatic in Greek mythology. As told by Apollodorus (*Library*, III, 4,5), Zeus had taken a fancy to Semele, one of the daughters of Cadmus, the hero who founded Thebes, and Harmonia, the daughter of Ares and Aphrodite. Jealous, Hera suggested to Semele that she ask her lover Zeus to appear to her in all his glory, as proof of his love. Zeus had promised Semele that he would grant anything she desired, and therefore could not deny her request. So he presented himself in all his splendor and power, with lightning and

thunderbolts, in a blaze of light that no mortal could withstand. Semele, six months pregnant, died as a result. But Zeus was able to remove the unborn child from her belly and place it inside his own thigh. Several months later Dionysus was born from the thigh of his father. To protect him from the anger of Hera, Zeus entrusted Dionysus to Ino, the sister of the unfortunate Semele and the wife of Athamus. The couple had two sons, Learches and Melicertes. But Hera, the jealous wife of Zeus, would not allow herself to be fooled, and, as punishment for taking in the child of his adulterous love affair, she caused Ino and Athamus to go mad. Athamus killed his son Learches with a spear, mistaking him for a stag. Ino killed Melicertes by placing him in boiling water and then threw herself into the sea while clutching his dead body. So Dionysus was forced to wander the earth in order to escape the persecution of Hera.

On his return to Greece, Dionysus went to Thebes, where the sisters of Semele had spread the word that he was not a son of Zeus, but the result of an adulterous relationship between his mother and some other man. At that time, Thebes was ruled by Pentheus, a cousin of Dionysus who was, like him, a descendent of Cadmus. First, Dionysus punished the women responsible for the calumny, putting them in a frenzy and causing them to go to Mount Cithaeron, on the outskirts of Thebes. Then he worked various wonders in order to convince Pentheus of his divine origin. But Pentheus, despite warnings from Cadmus and the seer Tiresias, took Dionysus for an imposter and was determined

Michelangelo Buonarroti
Caprese, Arezzo, 1475–Rome, 1564

Bacchus
c. 1496–1497

Marble
h. 72 ½ in (184 cm), base 80 in (203 cm)
Museum of the Bargello, Florence

Dionysus and the Maenads
Amphora
540–530 BC

Ceramic
h. 13 in (33 cm)
Bibliothèque National, Paris

to oppose him. Dionysus, however, persuaded him to climb Mount Cithaeron and to spy on the women from behind a pine tree, so that he could see their frenzied state for himself and so that he would know that it had been caused by Dionysus. Pentheus was discovered by the women and they, in the grip of their delirium, uprooted the pine tree and killed him, cutting him to pieces. His own mother, Agave, seized his head, thinking that it was the head of a lion, stuck it onto a thyrsus—a staff with ivy leaves at the top and one of the symbols of Dionysus—and carried it into the city, displaying it with pride. When she came to her senses, Agave realized that she had killed her own son. This is the main plot of *The Bacchae*, a tragedy by Euripides, and it was very popular in ancient art and literature.

In both ancient art and the art of modern times, the frenzy —"Dionysiac" or "orgiastic"—expressed in the myth is seen in the uncontrollable dance performed by the procession that follows Dionysus. It includes nymphs, sileni (creatures with the torso of a man and lower legs that end in horse hoofs, among which the musician Marsyas is often depicted), satyrs (creatures that are half-human and half-goat), as well as maenads and bacchantes (women in the grip of a frenzy). Among many possible examples of the Dionysiac dance, there is the very musical marble relief from Herculaneum (Naples, National Archaeological Museum) in which a maenad steps forward while playing a tambourine. She is followed by two satyrs which do not have the attributes of animals but which hold up some of the symbols

Angelica Kauffmann
Coira, 1741–
Rome, 1807
Ariadne Abandoned by Theseus, Discovered by Bacchus
1764
Oil on canvas
65 ¼ x 49 ¼ in
(166 x 125 cm)
Kulturamt der Landeshauptstadt, Bregenz

of Dionysus, such as a thyrsus and a lion skin, the lion being the animal into which Dionysus was transformed in the story of his voyage to Naxos (see below). As concerns the art of the modern era, the state of drunkenness and uncontrollable frenzy is expressed in an exemplary way by the fresco *The Triumph of Bacchus* from 1597–1602 by Annibale Carracci (Rome, Palazzo Farnese).

As with Agave in *The Bacchae* of Euripides, the madness and the frenzy are the fate of those who reject Dionysus, and of those who refuse to pay homage to him, with, eventually, the same fatal results as befell Pentheus. The orgiastic state was at the base of the celebrations in honor of Dionysus found all over the Greek world. One must keep in mind, however, that in ancient Greece the word "orgy" had the meaning of a rite performed as part of a religious mystery and that, despite its connection to a state of inebriation, the consumption of wine, and to dancing, all of which caused a person to lose his sense of order and routine, it did not have the sexual meaning that it has today.

Without forgetting its violent and vengeful character, one other episode regarding Dionysus narrated in the *Homeric Hymn to Dionysus* (no. VII) and recounted by Ovid in his *Metamorphoses* reminds us that he could also be sympathetic and appreciative. Dionysus had asked some Tyrrhenian pirates to take him to Naxos. Pretending to agree to his request, the pirates, who had mistaken him for the son of a king, tried to abduct Dionysus and take him to Asia.

The helmsman, recognizing his divine nature, warned his companions and asked them to free the youth immediately, but they did not listen. Then Dionysus caused wine to gush into the boat, transformed the oars into serpents, and caused vines and ivy to sprout and climb up the mast and spread everywhere. The pirates ordered the helmsman to bring the boat to shore, but Dionysus then transformed himself into a terrible lion and caused a bear to appear in the center of the ship, thereby revealing his divine nature. Terrified, the sailors threw themselves into the water and were transformed into dolphins. But Dionysus saved the helmsman who had tried to help him, and made him a happy and fortunate man.

This episode, among many examples, is the subject of two extraordinary Attic vases. On one, a black-figure kylix from around 530 BC made by Exekias (Munich, Staatliche Antikensammlung und Glyptothek), Dionysus is depicted on a narrow boat with sinuous grapevines that climb up the mast and spread to the left and right. From them hang seven bunches of grapes and there are seven dolphins that swim and jump under and at the sides of the ship. Here, all the transformations have already taken place and every element of this delicate, balanced, and flowing composition is more of a symbolic reference than a narration. In a detail on the other vase, a hydria from the 6th–5th century BC (Ohio, Toledo Museum of Art), we can see the moment in which the pirates are transformed into dolphins, in a composition that is as rhythmic as that on the first vase, if less refined.

Caravaggio (Michelangelo Merisi)
Caravaggio, Bergamo, 1571–Porto Ercole, Grosseto, 1610

Bacchus

c. 1599

Oil on canvas
37 ½ x 33 ½ in
(95 x 85 cm)
Uffizi Gallery, Florence

François Boucher
Paris, 1703–1770

Mercury Confiding the Infant Bacchus to the Nymphs

c. 1732–1734

Oil on canvas
90 ½ x 107 ½ in
(230 x 273 cm)
Wallace Collection, London

French school

The Birth of Bacchus

18th century

Oil on canvas
Musée Anne-de-Beaujeu, Moulins

The Childhood of Dionysus

1st century BC

Cameo in sardonic agate
1 ½ x 1 ¼ in
(4 x 3.3 cm)
National Archeological Museum, Naples

Dionysus and a Satyr

c. 150 BC

Marble relief
14 ¼ x 15 in
(36.5 x 38.5 cm)
National
Archeological
Museum,
Policoro

480

Dionysus

Workshop of Meidias

Dionysus and the Maenads

Detail from an Attic hydria

400–390 BC

Ceramic
h. 19 ½ in
(49.5 cm)
Badisches Landesmuseum, Karlsruhe

"BUT WHEN THE GODDESSES HAD BROUGHT HIM UP, A GOD OFT HYMNED,
THEN BEGAN HE TO WANDER CONTINUALLY THROUGH THE WOODY COOMBES,
THICKLY WREATHED WITH IVY AND LAUREL.
AND THE NYMPHS FOLLOWED IN HIS TRAIN WITH HIM FOR THEIR LEADER;
AND THE BOUNDLESS FOREST WAS FILLED WITH THEIR OUTCRY."

(*HOMERIC HYMNS*, XXVI,
"HYMN TO DIONYSUS," 6-9)

Dionysus with a Young Woman, a Maenad and a Satyr
Bell krater
Mid-4th century BC

Ceramic
h. 19 ½ in, diam. 19 in
(h. 50 cm, diam. 48 cm)
Soprintendenza Archeologica, Potenza

Dancing Maenads
Relief
I[st] century AD

Marble
Musée National
du Bardo,
Le Bardo

pp. 488–489

Dionysian Procession
Sarcophagus from a tomb on the Via Aurelia Antica
160–190 AD

Marble
h. 18 in, depth 22 in, breadth 77 in
(48 x 56 x 196 cm)
National Archeological Museum,
Naples

Dionysian Procession

2nd century AD

Mosaic
46 ¾ x 101 ½ in
(119 x 258 cm)
Musée National
du Bardo,
Le Bardo

pp. 492–493

Nicolas Poussin

Les Andelys, 1594–
Rome, 1665

Bacchanalia

c. 1627–1628

Oil on canvas
47 x 69 in
(121 x 175 cm)
Louvre,
Paris

pp. 494–495

Diego Velázquez
Seville, 1599–
Madrid, 1660

Triumph of Bacchus (The Drunkards)
c. 1628
Oil on canvas
65 x 88 ½ in
(165 x 225 cm)
Prado,
Madrid

"AROUND, THE BACCHAE, AND THE SATYRS THRONG;
BEHIND, SILENUS, DRUNK, LAGS SLOW ALONG.
ON HIS DULL ASS HE NODS FROM SIDE TO SIDE,
FORBEARS TO FALL, YET HALF FORGETS TO RIDE."

(OVID, *METAMORPHOSES*, IV)

Peter Paul Rubens
Siegen, 1577–Antwerp, 1640

Bacchus
1638–1640

Oil on canvas transferred from panel
75 ¼ x 63 ½ in (191 x 161.3 cm)
Hermitage,
St. Petersburg

Titian (Tiziano Vecellio)

Pieve di Cadore, Belluno, c. 1490–Venice, 1576

Bacchus and Ariadne

1520–1523

Oil on canvas
69 ½ x 75 ¼ in
(176.5 x 191 cm)
National Gallery, London

pp. 500–501

Annibale Carracci

Bologna, 1560–Rome, 1609

Triumph of Bacchus and Ariadne

c. 1597–1604

Fresco
Palazzo Farnese, Galleria Farnese, Rome

Alessandro Turchi (l'Orbetto)
Verona, c. 1578–Rome, c. 1650

Bacchus and Ariadne
c. 1630

Oil on canvas
44 3/4 x 58 in
(114 x 147.5 cm)
Hermitage,
St. Petersburg

Jacopo Amigoni

Naples, 1682-
Madrid, 1752

Bacchus and Ariadne

c. 1735

Oil on canvas
40 x 49 ½ in
(101.5 x 125.8 cm)
Walpole Gallery,
London

504

506

Dionysus

Exekias
Active c. 550–525 BC

Dionysus in a Boat with a Vine
Kylix
c. 530 BC

Ceramic
h. 5 ¼ in (13.6 cm)
diam. 12 in (30.5 cm)
Staatliche Antikensammlung und Glyptothek, Munich

"FIRST OF ALL SWEET, FRAGRANT WINE RAN STREAMING
THROUGHOUT ALL THE BLACK SHIP AND A HEAVENLY SMELL AROSE,
SO THAT ALL THE SEAMEN WERE SEIZED WITH AMAZEMENT WHEN THEY SAW IT.
AND ALL AT ONCE A VINE SPREAD OUT BOTH WAYS ALONG THE TOP OF THE SAIL
WITH MANY CLUSTERS HANGING DOWN FROM IT,
AND A DARK IVY-PLANT TWINED ABOUT THE MAST, BLOSSOMING WITH FLOWERS,
AND WITH RICH BERRIES GROWING ON IT;
AND ALL THE THOLE-PINS WERE COVERED WITH GARLANDS.
... BUT THE GOD CHANGED INTO A DREADFUL LION THERE ON THE SHIP ...
UNTIL SUDDENLY THE LION SPRANG UPON THE MASTER AND SEIZED HIM;
AND WHEN THE SAILORS SAW IT THEY LEAPT OUT OVERBOARD ONE AND ALL
INTO THE BRIGHT SEA,
ESCAPING FROM A MISERABLE FATE, AND WERE CHANGED INTO DOLPHINS."

(*HOMERIC HYMNS*, VII, "HYMN TO DIONYSUS," 35-53)

Demigods and Heroes

Bruges School

Cadmus

From Ovid's *Metamorphoses*, Ms 324, f. 35v.
Late 15th century

Miniature
9 x 7 ½ in
(23 x 19.2 cm)
Holkham Hall, Norfolk

The demigods are those born from the union of a god with a mortal woman, given supernatural powers but also human weaknesses. Heracles (known to the Romans as Hercules) belongs to this group of mythological figures. The heroes, on the other hand, are mortals who possess extraordinary ability and intelligence and rely on the protection of a god or goddess. In the case of Odysseus (the Romans Ulysses), in addition to his natural strength and shrewdness, he could count on the constant help of Athena (the Roman Minerva). Heroes are also of divine descent, even if not necessarily directly descended from one god. Odysseus, for example, had Zeus (or, according to another version, Kephalos) as a paternal great-grandfather and Hermes (the Roman Mercury) as a maternal great-grandfather.

There is a great difference between the legends of the heroes and the mythology of the gods. As Károly Kerényi says in his classic work *The Gods and the Heroes of Greece*, the distinction "between true mythology and the mythology of the heroes, between which there are many connections, consists in the fact that the mythology of the heroes is also more or less linked to history, to the events not of a 'primordial' era that exists outside of time but to 'historical' time, and is thus tightly intertwined with and relevant to that history, as if it were genuine history and not myth." The heroes and their deeds are characterized by surprising realism and their feelings are anything but idealized: they are clearly part of the human race.

Antoni Brodowski
Warsaw, 1784–1832

Oedipus and Antigone

1828

Oil on canvas
115 ¼ x 75 ¼ in
(293 x 191 cm)
Muzeum Narodowe, Warsaw

Nevertheless, again in the words of Kerényi, there falls on the hero "a 'light' which could, from the point of view of the history of religion, for which the divine is the presence from which that light originates, be called the splendor of the divine." The heroes give off that light even after death, and cults, altars, and tributes were dedicated to them, although to a lesser extent than to the gods.

In many cases, the heroes were associated with the founding of a city—this being, among others, one of their connections with history—and with its destiny. For this reason, works on mythology often refer to a body or group of myths and legends as a cycle, such as "the Theban cycle," about the history of Thebes, "the Mycenaean cycle," about the heroes connected to Mycenae, and "the Trojan cycle," about the Trojan war and the events preceding and subsequent to it. Sometimes, instead of being called a cycle, a group of myths and legends concerning a city or region is known as a saga. As an example, Cadmus, the legendary founder of Thebes, was the son of Agenor, who was the son of Poseidon and the great-grandson of Zeus. Cadmus was the father of Semele (the unlucky mother of the god Dionysus) and from him descended, among others, Creon, Jocasta, Oedipus, and Antigone. As a result, the myths concerning these heroes are closely linked to the city of Thebes and constitute "the Theban saga." In the epic poems as well as the tragedies, the emphasis is always on man, on his individual deeds and on the good and bad fortune that they inspire. So the celebratory aspect of the

Ajax Dragging Cassandra from the Cult Statue of Athena
Attic vase
5th century BCE
Ceramic
diam. 12 3/4 in (32.6 cm)
Louvre, Paris

founding of a city is of somewhat less importance, and, even if it is tied to a particular place, a heroic legend will cross the borders of its place of birth and spread to other areas of Greece and across the Mediterranean.

Art is not, however, concerned with these distinctions, first organized as dynastic cycles and territorial sagas by Apollodorus. They are connected more to the study of mythology than to the use of mythological subjects in the creation of art. Thus, in art, the heroes are often set apart and represented by their deeds more than by their association with a particular territory or dynasty, and by the dramatic nature of the stories told about them and the moral lessons that they embody. As for the legends handed down through the epic poems, the heroes most often depicted in both ancient art and modern art are Heracles, Perseus, Theseus, and the shrewd Odysseus, followed by Orpheus and Achilles. The Trojans Hector, Laocoon, and Aeneas have also received great attention. As a hero associated with the founding of Rome, Aeneas is found very often in Roman art as well as in modern Italian art. Among the women, the most popular is Ariadne, followed by Helen and Penelope. Among the tragic heroes, Oedipus is by far the one most favored by artists.

In the following pages many heroes are depicted, including some not mentioned above. For the various figures and their attributes, the reader may refer to the brief mythological dictionary at the end of this book.

Peter Paul Rubens

Siegen, 1577–
Antwerp, 1640

Cadmus Sowing the Dragon's Teeth

1636

Oil on panel
10 ½ x 16 ½ in
(26.7 x 42.2 cm)
Raveningham Hall,
Bacon Collection,
Norfolk

Francesco Zuccarelli

Pitigliano, Grosseto, 1702–Florence, 1788

Cadmus Killing the Dragon

1765

Oil on canvas
49 ¾ x 61 ¾ in
(126.4 x 157.2 cm)
Tate Gallery, London

Angelica
Kauffmann

Coira, 1741–
Rome, 1807

Ariadne Abandoned by Theseus

1774

Oil on canvas
25 x 35 ¾ in
(63.8 x 91 cm)
Museum of
Fine Arts,
Houston

520

James Barry
Cork, 1741–
London, 1806

The Education of Achilles

c. 1772

Oil on canvas
40 ½ x 50 ¾ in
(103 x 129 cm)
Yale Center for
British Art,
New Haven

522

Annibale Carracci

Bologna, 1560–
Rome, 1609

Perseus and Medusa

Lunette of the Camerino
c. 1595–1596

Fresco
Palazzo Farnese, Rome

Heracles

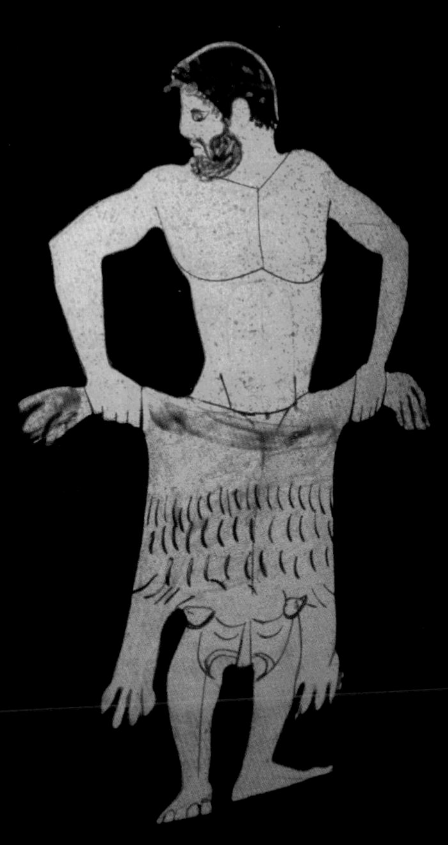

Heracles (or Herakles) is probably the best known hero from classical mythology and one of those who, since antiquity, have been favored by artists. He was known as Hercules by the Romans. His life and the legends that describe it are not, in a strict sense, a single myth, so much as a heroic cycle, according to the critic Pierre Grimal. A myth is usually based on a particular view of the universe and of life, and it has a religious dimension that is not present in the figure of Heracles. A heroic cycle is, instead, characterized by stories "whose sole unity is provided by the identity of the figure who is the main hero." The most famous of his many adventures are those which, over time and in the work of those who wrote down the myths, from pre-Hellenistic times through late antiquity, have become known as the Twelve Labors of Heracles.

According to Homer, Heracles was the son of Zeus and Alcmene, the wife of Amphitryon. Taking advantage of the absence of Amphitryon, Zeus disguised himself as Amphitryon and slept with Alcmene. Thus was born the demigod Heracles, who had both incomparable strength and a hot-tempered personality. As with all the other lovers taken by Zeus and the resulting children, Hera bore a grudge against Heracles, who had to endure her persecution. In a fit of madness caused in him by Hera, Heracles killed the three children that he had with Megara, the daughter of the king of Thebes. The oracle of Delphi decided that Heracles, in order to atone for his sin, had to place himself in the service of Eurystheus, the king of

Berlin Painter

Heracles and the Serpents with Athena
Attic vase
Early 5th century BC
Ceramic
h. 20 in (51 cm)
Louvre, Paris

Heracles with Lion Skin and an Athlete
Amphora
490 BC
Ceramic
Bibliothèque Nationale de France, Cabinet des Médailles, Paris

Tiryns, who imposed the famous twelve labors on him. Among these, Heracles had to confront the lion of Nemea, an animal of extraordinary size and ferocity, free the city of Lerna from the Hydra, a serpent with nine heads, and capture Cerberus, a dog with three heads that guarded the entrance to Hades, the kingdom of the dead.

The labors of Heracles, along with the other legends linked to him, were depicted as early as the 7th century BC, when the technique of black-figure decoration appeared on Greek pottery. At that time and during later centuries, the gods and heroes were rendered as black figures with engraved outlines on a red-yellow clay background, in compositions almost certainly inspired by pictorial works such as paintings and frescoes that are now lost but which are known through literary sources. Among many examples, an Attic amphora from the 6th century BC with *The Dispute over the Keryneian Hind between Heracles, Apollo, and Artemis under the eye of Athena* (Vatican City, Vatican Museums) stands out, along with two amphoras from the beginning of the 5th century BC with *Heracles Strikes the Hydra of Lerna with an Axe* and *Heracles Fights the Birds of Stymphalos* (Paris, the Louvre). These two amphoras clearly show the traditional attributes of the hero: a lion skin (from the lion of Nemea) and a club. At times, the demigod is also depicted with a sword, which was a gift from Hermes, or with a bow and arrow, given by Apollo.

The second half of the 6th century BC sees the first red-

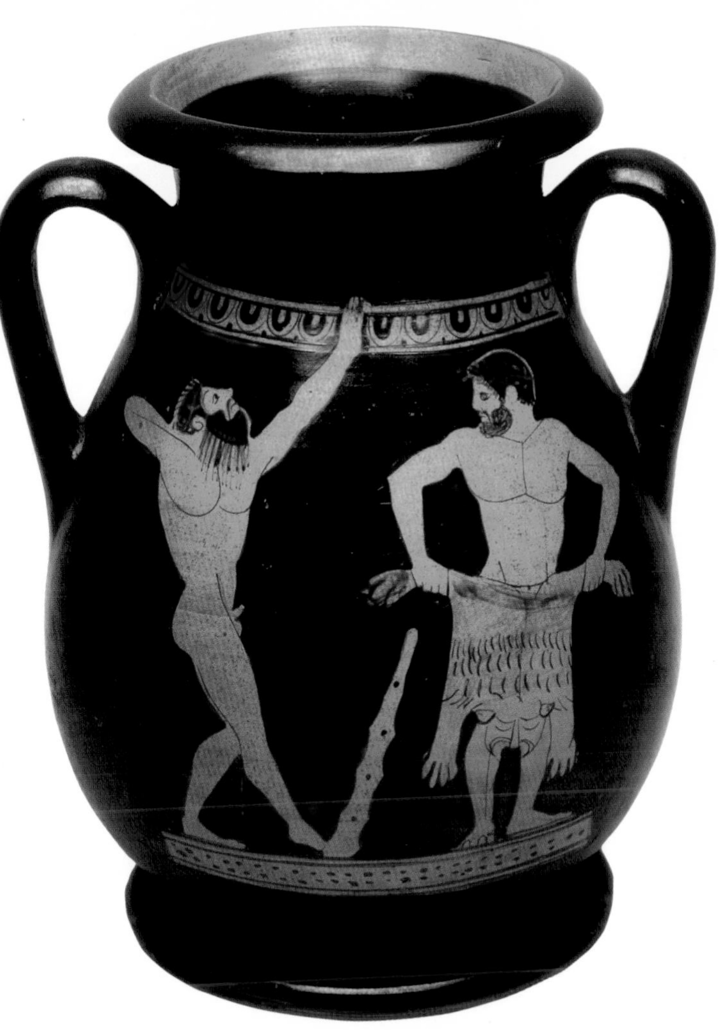

figure vases, which have black lines within red figures on a black background. With this technique, for around a century, the vase painters were able to show not only the foreshortening of the figures but also to render spatial depth and the psychological expression of the characters. Among the most important examples of this style as applied to the figure of Heracles are a calyx krater (a large vase used to mix wine and water at banquets) from around 510 BC depicting his struggle with Antaios, painted by Euphronios, and a jug with *The Child Heracles kills the Two Serpents* from around 480 BC (Paris, the Louvre).

Glycon from Athens
Active 2nd–3rd century AD

Farnese Heracles
From the Baths of Caracalla, Rome
Copy from an original 4th-century BC bronze attributed to Lysippus
Early 3rd century

Marble
h. 125 in (317 cm)
National Archeological Museum, Naples

There are many depictions of Heracles in ancient sculpture. Two of the most interesting are the *Lansdowne Heracles* (Malibu, J. Paul Getty Foundation) and the *Farnese Heracles*, which was found in the Baths of Caracalla (Naples, National Archeological Museum). Both are from the 4th century BC and show the hero with his club and the lion skin, symbols of his strength and of the twelve labors. There are also many Greek, Roman, and Etruscan mosaics that illustrate his feats.

The figure of Heracles remained a popular theme for artists and patrons up until the first centuries of the Christian era. It disappeared as an artistic theme in the centuries that followed, along with many other mythological subjects. One of its last appearances in ancient art is on a 1st-century wall painting from Herculaneum called *Heracles Strangles the Serpents* (Naples, National Archeological Museum).

Antonio del Pollaiolo
Florence, c. 1432–Rome, 1498

Heracles and Antaeus
c. 1475

Tempera on panel
6 1/4 x 3 1/2 in
(16 x 9 cm)
Uffizi Gallery,
Florence

534

Like many other gods and heroes of classical mythology, Heracles would reappear in art during the 15th century, in Florence. The sculptor and painter Antonio del Pollaiolo was one of the first, in modern times, to make use of subjects that were strictly mythological. Around 1460, at the request of Lorenzo the Magnificent, he painted three large canvases depicting the labors of Heracles, but they have been lost. Two small panels by Pollaiolo titled *Heracles and the Hydra* and *Heracles and Antaios* (Florence, Uffizi Gallery) are thought to be based on those works. We no longer see the same linear style or two-color aesthetic of the depictions on antique vases, but rather a surrender to the plasticity of the figures, especially with regard to their anatomy, that was more than just a reminder of the powerful masculine figures of antique sculpture, which was being rediscovered over the course of the 1400s. The scenes are full of energy, thanks to the sinewy outlines that make up the figures of Heracles and his opponents. In *Heracles and the Hydra*, the lion skin swells in front of the hero during his energetic bounce, and the tail of his cloak forms a curve, like the Hydra's many long necks and like its tail which wraps around one of Heracles' legs. In addition, the scenes are not silhouetted in an abstract way against a monochrome background, but are set in a landscape that goes as far as the eye can see, under the influence of Flemish painting and the study of perspective.

By now understood as an incarnation of good which triumphs over evil, according to a Neoplatonic inter-

Peter Paul Rubens
Siegen, 1577–Antwerp, 1640

Heracles in the Garden of Hesperides
c. 1638
Oil on canvas
95 ½ x 56 ½ in
(242 x 144 cm)
Galleria Sabauda, Turin

pretation of his legend, Heracles once again became a popular subject and would remain one over time. Pollaiolo again depicted *Heracles and Antaios* in a small bronze from around 1470 (Florence, Museo del Bargello). Vincenzo de' Rossi, a 16th century sculptor from Florence, presented his version of the subject in a sculptural group that today is found in that city's Palazzo Vecchio. In 1599, also for the municipality of Florence, Giambologna carved a group in marble with *Heracles and the Centaur Nessus*. Some years later, Rubens painted *Heracles Fights the Nemean Lion* (Bucharest, Rumanian National Museum of Art) and *Heracles in the Garden of the Hesperides* (Turin, Galleria Sabauda). The Spanish painter Francisco de Zurbarán produced a version with tenebrist effects that shows the hero confronting the dog that guarded the entrance to the Underworld, *Heracles and Cerberus* (Madrid, Museo del Prado). Somewhat later, in the early 1800s, the sculptor Antonio Canova made the most of the theme of the anger of Heracles in a sculptural group of great dramatic force that depicts the hero hurling his friend Lycus into the air (Possagno, Gipsoteca Canoviana). There is also a version of an episode in the life of the hero that falls somewhere between the fantastic and the phantasmagoric, a painting from 1869–1876 by Gustave Moreau called *Heracles and the Hydra of Lerna*. It would be a mistake, however, to attribute the popularity of the hero with artists only to the symbolic idea of good that triumphs over evil. Perhaps, more than anything else, artists have been interested in the dramatic and exasperated nature of his adventures.

The Lansdowne Heracles

Roman copy from a Greek original dated 4th century BC

c. 125 AD

Marble
h. 76 in (193.5 cm)
J. Paul Getty Museum,
Malibu

Infant Heracles Strangling Serpents Sent by Juno

1st century AD

Fresco in 4th style
Casa dei Vettii,
Pompeii

Heracles

Heracles Killing his Music Teacher
Kylix
470 BC

Ceramic
Bibliothèque Nationale de France,
Cabinet des Médailles
Paris

pp. 546–547

The Labors of Heracles

Detail from a sarcophagus
2nd century AD

Marble
29 x 89 in
(73.7 x 225.8 cm)
Palazzo Ducale,
Mantua

"HAVING FIRST LEARNED FROM EURYTHUS
THE ART OF ARCHERY,
HERACLES RECEIVED A SWORD FROM HERMES,
A BOW AND ARROWS FROM APOLLO,
A GOLDEN BREASTPLATE FROM HEPHAESTUS,
AND A ROBE FROM ATHENA;
FOR HE HAD HIMSELF CUT A CLUB AT NEMEA."

(APOLLODORUS, *LIBRARY*, II, 4, 11)

Labor of Heracles

Calyx krater
5th century BC

Ceramic
Louvre,
Paris

Heracles Battling the Nemean Lion

Attic anphora

c. 6th century BC

Ceramic
Ashmolean
Museum,
Oxford

548

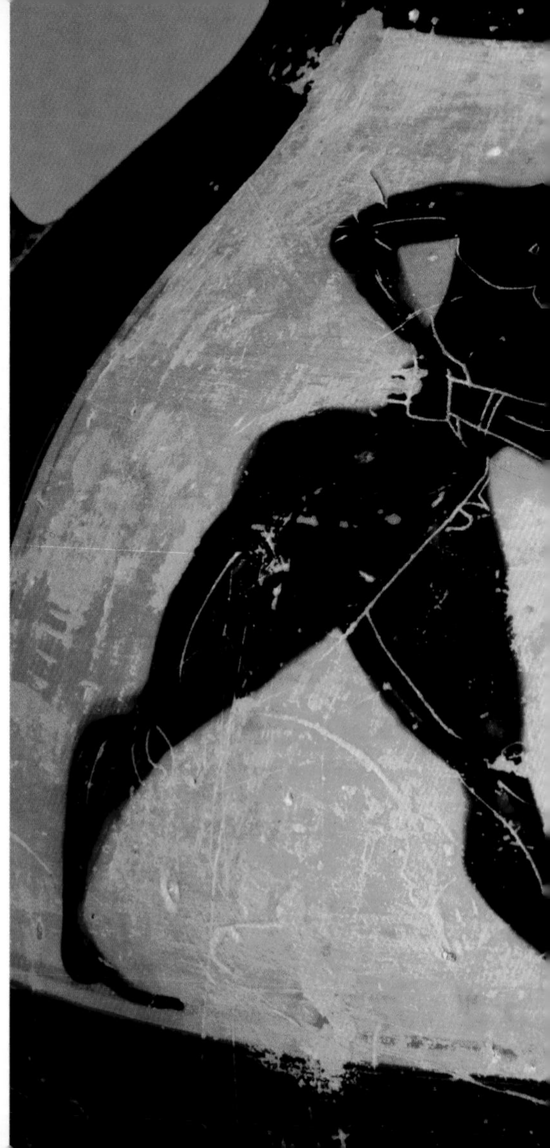

Pier Jacopo Alari Bonacolsi (l'Antico)

Mantua, c. 1460–Gazzuolo, Mantua, 1528

Heracles and the Nemean Lion

c. 1490

Bronze
Diam. 12 ¾ in (32.7 cm)
Museum of the Bargello, Florence

Peter Paul Rubens

Siegen, 1577–
Antwerp, 1640

Hercules Strangling the Nemean Lion

1638–39

Oil on panel
9 x 15 ½ in
(23 x 39.2 cm)
Private collection,
St. Louis

Diosphos Painter

Active early 5th century BC

Heracles and the Hydra

Ceramic
Louvre,
Paris

554

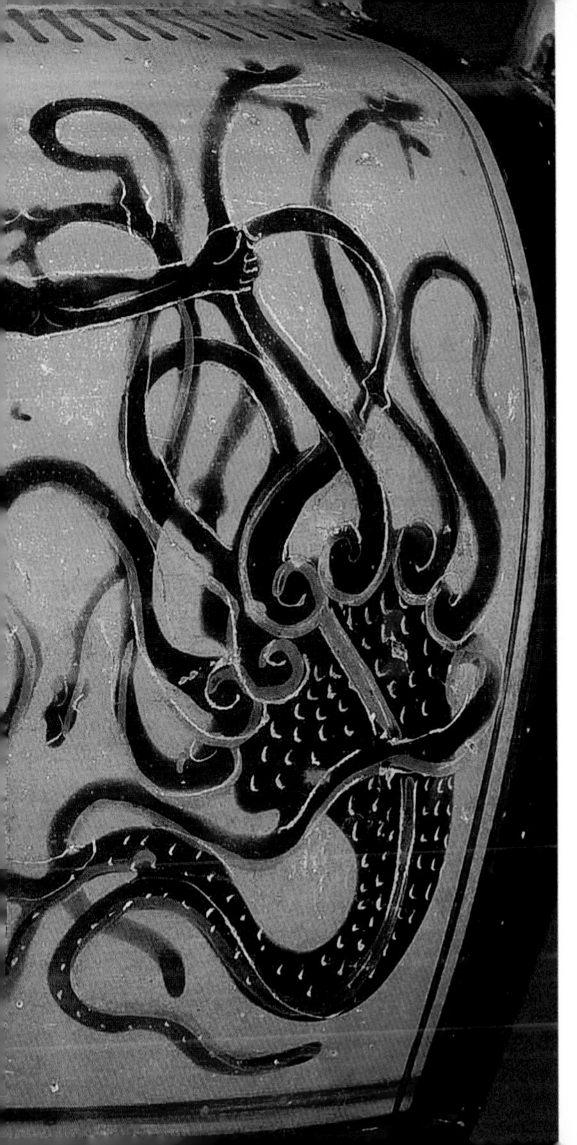

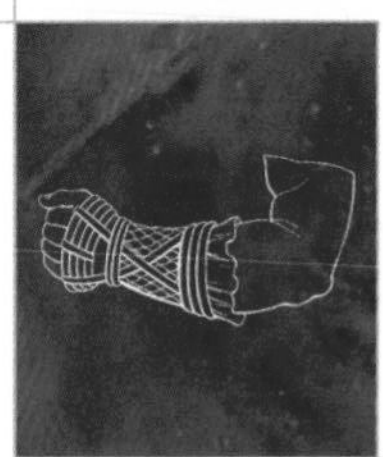

Heracles Killing the Hydra

c. 320–350 AD

Fresco
Catacombs of the via Latina,
Catacomb in via Dino Compagni,
Rome

"HE DISCOVERED THE HYDRA ON A HILL BESIDE THE SPRINGS OF THE AMYMONE, WHERE WAS ITS DEN. BY PELTING IT WITH FIERY SHAFTS HE FORCED IT TO COME OUT, AND IN THE ACT OF DOING SO HE SEIZED AND HELD IT FAST.
BUT THE HYDRA WOUND ITSELF ABOUT ONE OF HIS FEET AND CLUNG TO HIM.
NOR COULD HE EFFECT ANYTHING BY SMASHING ITS HEADS WITH HIS CLUB, FOR AS FAST AS ONE HEAD WAS SMASHED THERE GREW UP TWO."

(APOLLODORUS, *LIBRARY*, II, 5, 2)

Antonio del Pollaiolo
Florence, c. 1432–Rome, 1498

Heracles and the Hydra

c. 1475

Tempera on panel
6 ½ x 4 ¾ in (17 x 12 cm)
Uffizi Gallery,
Florence

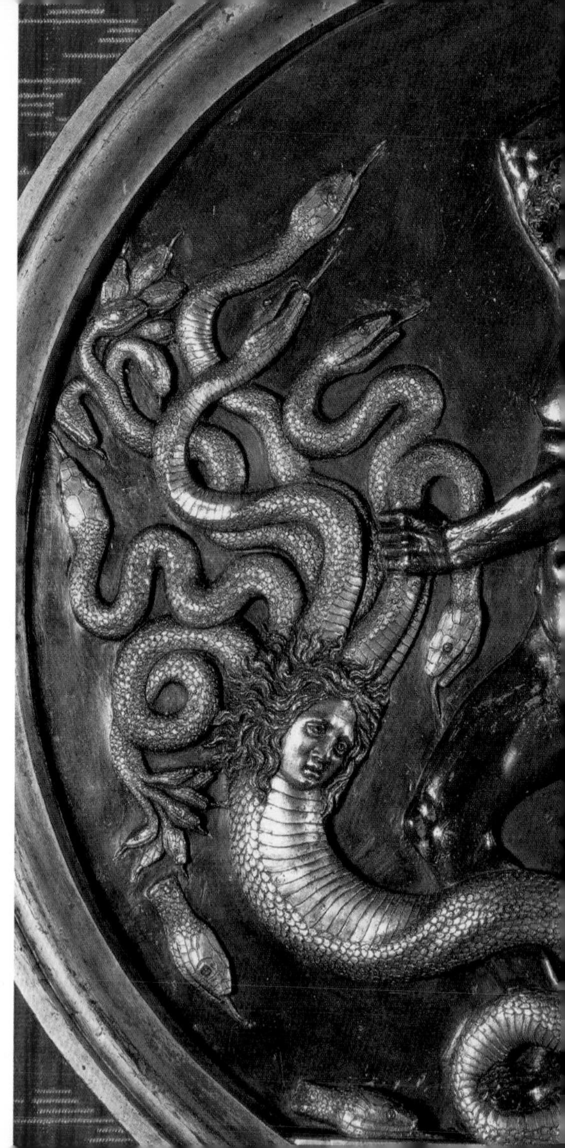

Pier Jacopo Alari Bonacolsi (l'Antico)

Mantua, c. 1460–Gazzuolo, Mantua, 1528

Heracles and the Hydra

c. 1490

Bronze medal
diam. 12 ¾ in (32.7 cm)
Museum of the Bargello, Florence

562

Heracles

Narcisse Berchère
1819–1891

Heracles and the Lernaean Hydra
after Gustave Moreau
c. 1876

Oil on canvas
21 ½ x 17 ¾ in
(55 x 45 cm)
Musée Gustave Moreau,
Paris

Heracles and the Cretan Bull

Detail
from Ostia

Early 2nd century

Mosaic
22 ½ x 22 ½ in
(57 x 57 cm)
Czartoryski
Museum,
Cracow

Andokides Painter
Active c. 530-515 BC

Hercules and Cerberus
Amphora
c. 530–520 BC

Ceramic
h. 23 in (58.2 cm)
Louvre,
Paris

Francisco
de Zurbarán

Fuente de Cantos,
1598–Madrid, 1664

**Heracles
and Cerberus**

1634

Oil on canvas
52 x 59 ½ in
(132 x 151 cm)
Prado,
Madrid

568

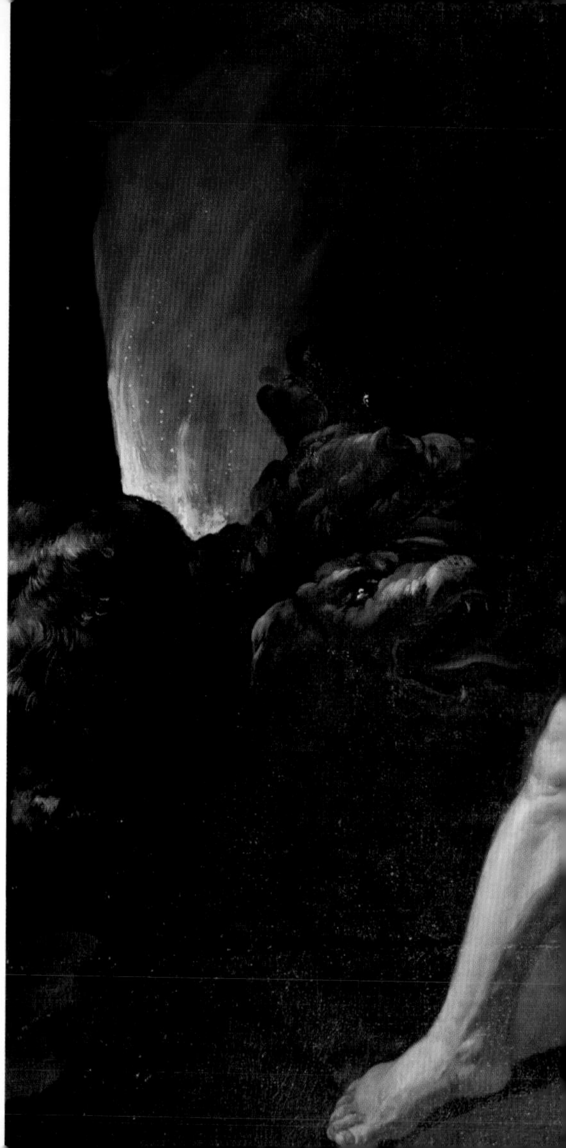

Heracles

Euphronios
Active c. 520–500 BC

Heracles and Antaeus
Attic krater from Cerveteri
c. 515–510 BC
Ceramic
h. 17 ½ in
(44.8 cm)
Louvre
Paris

"BEING FORCED TO WRESTLE WITH HIM,
HERACLES HUGGED HIM,
LIFTED HIM ALOFT, BROKE AND KILLED HIM;
FOR WHEN HE TOUCHED EARTH SO IT WAS
THAT HE WAXED STRONGER,
WHEREFORE SOME SAID THAT HE WAS A SON
OF EARTH."

(APOLLODORUS, *LIBRARY*, II, 5, 11)

Antonio del Pollaiolo
Florence, 1432–Rome, 1498

Heracles and Antaeus

c. 1475

Bronze
h. 17 ¾ in (45 cm)
Museum of the Bargello,
Florence

Hans Baldung Grien

Schwäbisch Gmünd c. 1484–Strasbourg, 1545

Heracles and Antaeus

1530

Oil on panel
39 x 28 ½ in
(98.8 x 72.7 cm)
Muzeum Narodowe, Warsaw

Pierre Reymond

Limoges, c. 1513–c. 1584

The Labors of Heracles

Limoges saltcellar

Mid 16th century

Enamel on copper
h. 3 ¼ in (8.2 cm)
Louvre,
Paris

Jean de Boulogne (Giambologna)

Douai, 1529–Florence, 1608

Heracles and the Centaur Nessus

c. 1599

Marble
Loggia dei Lanzi, Florence

pp. 580–581

David
Vinckboons

Malines, 1576–
Amsterdam, 1629

**Heracles,
Deianira, and
the Centaur
Nessus**

1612

Oil on panel
28 x 36 ½ in
(71.5 x 92.5 cm)
Kunsthistorisches
Museum,
Vienna

"AND TAKING DEIANIRA WITH HIM, HE CAME TO THE RIVER EVENUS,
AT WHICH THE CENTAUR NESSUS SAT
AND FERRIED PASSENGERS ACROSS FOR HIRE,
ALLEGING THAT HE HAD RECEIVED THE FERRY FROM THE GODS FOR HIS RIGHTEOUSNESS.
SO HERACLES CROSSED THE RIVER BY HIMSELF,
BUT ON BEING ASKED TO PAY THE FARE
HE ENTRUSTED DEIANIRA TO NESSUS TO CARRY OVER.
BUT HE, IN FERRYING HER ACROSS,
ATTEMPTED TO VIOLATE HER.
SHE CRIED OUT, HERACLES HEARD HER,
AND SHOT NESSUS TO THE HEART
WHEN HE EMERGED FROM THE RIVER."

(APOLLODORUS, *THE LIBRARY*, II, 7, 6)

Guido Reni
Bologna, 1575–1642

The Abduction of Deianira

1617–1621

Oil on canvas
94 x 76 in (239 x 193 cm)
Louvre,
Paris

Louis Jean François Lagrenée

Paris, c. 1724–1805

The Rape of Deianira

1755

Oil on canvas
61 ¾ x 72 ¾ in
(157 x 185 cm)
Louvre,
Paris

Arnold Böcklin

Basel, 1827 –
San Domenico,
Florence, 1901

Deianira and Nessus

1898

Oil on panel
41 x 59 in
(104 x 150 cm)
Pfalzgalerie,
Kaiserslautern

Francisco
de Zurbarán

Fuente de Cantos,
1598–Madrid, 1664

**The Death
of Heracles**

1634

Oil on canvas
53 ½ x 65 ¾ in
(136 x 167 cm)
Prado,
Madrid

"... 'LYCHAS, TO THEE ALONE MY FATE I OWE,
WHO BORE THE GIFT, THE CAUSE OF ALL MY WOE!'
THE YOUTH ALL PALE, WITH SHIVERING FEAR WAS STUNG,
AND VAIN EXCUSES FALTERED ON HIS TONGUE.
ALCIDES SNATCHED HIM, AS WITH SUPPLIANT FACE
HE STROVE TO CLASP HIS KNEES, AND BEG FOR GRACE:
HE TOSSED HIM OVER HIS HEAD WITH AIRY COURSE,
AND HURLED WITH MORE THAN WITH AN ENGINE'S FORCE
FAR OVER THE EUBAEAN MAIN ALOOF HE FLIES,
AND HARDENS BY DEGREES AMID THE SKIES."

(OVID, *METAMORPHOSES*, IX)

Antonio Canova
Possagno, Treviso, 1757–Venice, 1822

Heracles and Lichas
1795–1815

Marble
h. 138 in (350 cm)
Galleria Nazionale d'Arte Moderna, Rome

Luca Giordano

Naples, 1634-1705

Heracles on the Funeral Pyre

1697–1700

Oil on canvas
49 ¼ x 31 ½ in (125 x 80 cm)
Monastero di San Lorenzo,
El Escorial

Perseus

Benvenuto Cellini
Florence, 1500–1571

Perseus with the Head of Medusa
1545–1554

Bronze
h. c. 126 in
(320 cm)
Loggia dei Lanzi,
Florence

Perseus is another hero often favored by artists and their patrons. Depicted at least as early as the 7th century BC, Perseus and the mythological figures linked to him, such as Medusa and Andromeda, were portrayed again in the 1500s. He is the subject of one of the most important sculptures of the Renaissance, the monumental *Perseus with the Head of Medusa* by Benvenuto Cellini (Florence, Loggia dei Lanzi). Another great exploit by Perseus is the subject of an extraordinary painting by Piero di Cosimo, *Perseus Frees Andromeda*, from around 1513–15 (Florence, Uffizi Gallery).

The ancient authors, with some exceptions, were more or less in agreement concerning the birth of Perseus and the episodes that make up his legend. Once again, the most complete narratives about the hero are found in Apollodorus (*Library*, II, 4) and Ovid (*Metamorphoses*, IV, 617). Many passages and individual episodes are confirmed by other authors, for example the decapitation of Medusa, mentioned by Hesiod (*Theogony*, 276–279) and Pindar (*Pythian Odes*, X, 31), and the story of his birth, by, among others, Sophocles (*Antigone*, 944–955).

The story of Perseus repeats a motif found often in Greek mythology, that of a prophesy according to which the birth of a baby would bring about the death of its father or grandfather. Akrisios, the king of Argos, had gone to Delphi to consult the famous oracle, which predicted this fate. In order to avoid the prophesy, Akrisios locked his daughter Danae in an underground room made of bronze that he built under the

Danae in a Chest Washed Ashore on the Island of Serifos
Detail of an Attic kylix
5th century BC
Ceramic
Museo Spina, Ferrara

courtyard of his palace, so that she could not become pregnant and bear a son who would kill him. But this was not enough to keep Zeus, who was captivated by her beauty, from entering the armored chamber in the form of a shower of gold, and he impregnated her. With the help of her maidservant, Danae gave birth to a boy, Perseus, and she hid him from her father. Nevertheless, Akrisios discovered what happened and, not wanting to believe his daughter, who said that she had been seduced by a god, he put mother and child in a chest and threw it into the sea, in order to free himself from his small grandson and the risk of being killed. But the sea carried the chest to the island of Seriphos, where the abandoned mother and child were found by a fisherman, Diktys, the brother of the local king, Polydektes. An ancient cup from the 5th century BC (Comacchio, Spina Museum) shows the arrival of Danae and her son on Seriphos and their rescue by the fisherman.

Diktys took them into his home and raised the boy. Meanwhile, Danae had aroused, despite herself, the desires of Polydektes, who was unable to possess her because Perseus, by now a very beautiful and strong youth, guarded his mother. So Polydektes devised a strategy to distract him. He invited Perseus and other friends to a meal and asked what they intended to give him as a gift for his wedding to Hippodamia. All of them answered that the gift most suited to a king would be a horse. Perseus, raised by a fisherman, could not make such a gift and said that he would, if desired by Polydektes, bring him the head of Medusa, one of the Gorgons, frightful monsters who turned to stone anyone who looked them in the eyes. Polydektes then

Gorgon
Detail of an Attic kylix
c. 500 BC
Ceramic
Ashmolean Museum, Oxford

demanded that Perseus keep his promise and Perseus had to go in hunt of the monster. Counseled by Hermes and Athena, Perseus searched for Medusa who, with her two sisters, lived far to the west, beyond the ocean, where, it was believed, the kingdom of the dead was located. For this purpose, Hermes gave Perseus an extremely strong sickle and the Nymphs lent him a knapsack, a pair of winged sandals, and the helmet of Hades, which made its wearer invisible. Perseus came upon the three Gorgons—Sthenno, Euryale, and Medusa—while they were sleeping. Athough the Gorgons inspired fear even in the gods, Poseidon had nevertheless mated with Medusa and made her pregnant. Of the three Gorgons, only Medusa was mortal. Perseus threw himself on her and cut off her head. At that moment, the two creatures born from the union of Medusa and Poseidon—the winged horse Pegasus and Chrysaor, a man with a sword made of gold—sprang out from her neck. When he returned to Seriphos, Perseus learned that Polydektes had tried to seize Danae by force and that his mother and his adopted father Diktys had taken refuge at various altars which, being sacred places, were inviolable. In order to take revenge on Polydektes and his accomplices, Perseus exposed them to the gaze of Medusa's severed head and turned them to stone.

Medusa is one of the monsters of classical mythology most often depicted in the history of art. But if in ancient art her depictions do resemble in some ways the descriptions of the ancient authors—that is, a feminine creature with serpents on the head instead of hair, teeth similar to the tusks of boars, scales covering the neck, hands made of bronze, and wings of

gold—in modern art she retains only the serpent head of hair. This shows that the use of mythology in art is not only for illustrative purposes but has free rein and often even contradicts the ancient sources. To see this, one need only compare some ancient plates that depict the heads of the Gorgons with the famous *Medusa* by Caravaggio (Florence, Uffizzi Gallery) from around 1596–98 and the *Head of Medusa* by Peter Paul Rubens (Vienna, Kunsthistorisches Museum) from some twenty years later. On the other hand, it is obvious that the *Medusa* of Caravaggio, painted on a round board in the shape of a convex shield, reminds us that, at the end of his heroic saga, Perseus gave the head of the monster to the goddess Athena, who attached it to her own shield and used it as a deadly weapon against her enemies.

But, before giving the head of Medusa to Athena, Perseus took part in another adventure. On his way back to Seriphos, Perseus passed through Ethiopia, where he came upon Andromeda, the daughter of Kepheus, the king. She had been bound to a rock and exposed to a sea monster because her mother Kassiopeia had been foolish enough to challenge the Nereids to a beauty contest. The sea goddesses—among them Thetis, the mother of Achilles, Amphitrite, the wife of Poseidon, and Galatea, who was desired by the Cyclops Polyphemos—were offended and asked Poseidon to avenge them. So Poseidon, the sea god, sent a devastating flood and a sea monster, and a local oracle revealed that the only way to free the land from this scourge was to give Andromeda to be devoured by the monster. Perseus told Kepheus that he

Lord Frederic Leighton
Scarborough, Yorkshire, 1830–London, 1896

Perseus on Pegasus Hastening to the Rescue of Andromeda
1895

Oil on canvas
10 ½ x 10 ½ in
(27 x 26.7 cm)
Sotheby's, London

Giorgio Vasari
Arezzo, 1511–Florence, 1574

Perseus and Andromeda
1570–1572

Oil on slate
44 3/4 x 34 in
(113.9 x 86.4 cm)
Palazzo Vecchio, Florence

would free Andromeda, on the condition that he be allowed to marry her. Kepheus accepted and Perseus returned the girl to her parents, but the wedding with Andromeda was delayed because of yet another difficulty. She had been promised to her uncle Phineus and when he found out about the agreement between his brother and Perseus he organized a plot against the hero. But Perseus, still in possession of the head of Medusa, turned Phineus and his accomplices to stone.

In relation to this story of the freeing of Andromeda, we have already mentioned the painting by Piero di Cosimo. The dramatic struggle of Perseus against Phineus and his companions is the theme of a painting by Luca Giordano from around 1680 (London, National Gallery) in which the hero holds up the head of Medusa and uses it as a weapon.

The saga of Perseus closes with his return to Argos, the land of his birth. As told by Apollodorus (*Library*, II, 4) the hero wished to see his grandfather Akrisios once again. But learning that Perseus was about to arrive in Argos, Akrisios fled to the land of the Pelasgians, where Teutamidas, the king of Larissa, had organized commemorative games in honor of his dead father. Perseus went there to compete in the pentathlon. Akrisios was in the crowd in disguise. When he hurled the discus, Perseus accidentally hit him, causing his death. In this way the oracle uttered by Pythia at Delphi was fulfilled. Disconsolate, Perseus did not dare to claim the throne of Argos, which was rightfully his, and exchanged it for that of Tiryns, whose king was his cousin Megapenthes.

"WHEN ACRISIUS INQUIRED OF THE ORACLE
HOW HE SHOULD GET MALE CHILDREN,
THE GOD SAID THAT HIS DAUGHTER WOULD
GIVE BIRTH TO A SON
WHO WOULD KILL HIM.
FEARING THAT, ACRISIUS BUILT A BRAZEN
CHAMBER UNDER GROUND,
AND THERE GUARDED DANAE.
HOWEVER, SHE WAS SEDUCED, AS SOME SAY,
BY PROTEUS, WHENCE AROSE THE QUARREL
BETWEEN THEM.
BUT SOME SAY THAT ZEUS HAD
INTERCOURSE WITH HER
IN THE SHAPE OF A STREAM OF GOLD,
WHICH POURED THROUGH THE ROOF INTO
DANAE'S LAP."

(APOLLODORUS, *LIBRARY*, II, 4, 1)

pp. 608-609

Titian (Tiziano Vecellio)
Pieve di Cadore, Belluno, c. 1490–Venice, 1576

Danae
1545–1546

Oil on canvas
47 1/4 x 67 3/4 in (120 x 172 cm)
National Museum of Capodimonte, Naples

Mabuse (Jan Gossaert)
Maubeuge, c. 1478–Middelburg, 1532

Danae
1527

Oil on panel
45 x 37 1/2 in (114.2 X 95.4 cm)
Alte Pinakothek,
Munich

Jacques Berger

Danae and Perseus Saved by the Corsals on the Island of Serifos

19th century

Oil on canvas
65 ¾ x 92 in
(167 x 234 cm)
Accademia di Brera,
Milan

“AND WHILE ATHENA GUIDED HIS HAND,
HE LOOKED WITH AVERTED GAZE ON A BRAZEN SHIELD,
IN WHICH HE BEHELD THE IMAGE OF THE GORGON,
HE BEHEADED HER.”

(APOLLODORUS, *LIBRARY*, II, 4, 2

Perseus and the Gorgon
Metope from Selinus C Temple
530 BC

Marble
h. 58 in (147 cm)
Regional Archeological Museum, Palermo

Perseus and Medusa
Attic stamnos
6th–5th century BC

Ceramic
British Museum, London

614

"BUT THE GORGONS HAD HEADS TWINED ABOUT WITH THE SCALES OF DRAGONS, AND GREAT TUSKS LIKE SWINE'S, AND BRAZEN HANDS,
AND GOLDEN WINGS, BY WHICH THEY FLEW; AND THEY TURNED TO STONE SUCH AS BEHELD THEM."

(APOLLODORUS, *LIBRARY*, II, 4, 2)

Peter Paul Rubens
Siegen, 1577–Antwerp, 1640

Head of Medusa
Detail
c. 1617

Oil on panel
27 1/4 x 46 1/2 in (69.5 x 118 cm)
Kunsthistorisches Museum,
Vienna

Odilon Redon

Bordeaux, 1840–
Paris, 1916

Pegasus

1914

Oil on canvas
22 ¾ x 20 in
(58 x 51 cm)
Gemeentemuseum,
The Hague

Perseus Saving Andromeda

Relief found in Piazza SS. Apostoli, in Rome

Late 1st century AD

Marble
Musei Capitolini,
Rome

Perseus and Andromeda

From Dioscures House, Pompeii

69–96 AD

Wall painting in 4th style
38 ½ x 47 ¼ in
(98 x 120 cm)

National Archeological Museum, Naples

622

Perseus

"BEING COME TO ETHIOPIA, OF WHICH
CEPHEUS WAS KING,
HE FOUND THE KING'S DAUGHTER
ANDROMEDA
SET OUT TO BE THE PREY OF A SEA MONSTER.
FOR CASSIEPEA, THE WIFE OF CEPHEUS,
VIED WITH THE NEREIDS IN BEAUTY
AND BOASTED TO BE BETTER THAN THEM ALL;
HENCE THE NEREIDS WERE ANGRY,
AND POSEIDON, SHARING THEIR WRATH,
SENT A FLOOD AND A MONSTER TO INVADE
THE LAND."

(APOLLODORUS, *LIBRARY*, II, 4, 3)

Master of the City of the Ladies
(and scholars)

Perseus and Andromeda

From *Collected Works of Christine de Pisan*,
Ms. Harley 4431, f. 98v
1410–1411

Miniature
c. 4 ¼ x 3 in (11 x 8 cm)
British Library,
London

pp. 626–627

Piero di Cosimo

Florence,
1461–1521

Perseus Freeing Andromeda

c. 1515

Oil on panel
28 x 48 ½ in
(71 x 123 cm)
Uffizi Gallery,
Florence

Titian

(Tiziano Vecellio)

Pieve di Cadore, Belluno, c. 1490–Venice, 1576

Perseus and Andromeda

c. 1553–1562

Oil on canvas
69 x 74 ½ in
(175 x 189.5 cm)
Wallace Collection, London

Peter Paul Rubens

Siegen, 1577–Antwerp, 1640

Perseus and Andromeda

c. 1622

Oil on canvas
39 x 54 ¾ in
(99.5 x 139 cm)
Hermitage,
St. Petersburg

Abraham van Cuylenborch
Utrecht, 1610–1658

Perseus and Andromeda

c. 1652

Oil on panel
11 ³/₄ x 15 in
(30 x 38 cm)
Kunsthandel
Schloss Ahlden

pp. 634–635

Charles Antoine Coypel
Paris, 1694–1752

Perseus Rescuing Andromeda

1727

Oil on canvas
51 ¹/₂ x 77 in
(131 x 196 cm)
Louvre,
Paris

Edward Coley Burne-Jones

Birmingham, 1833–Fulham, London, 1898

Perseus Slaying the Sea Serpent

1876

Gouache on paper
60 ½ x 54 ½ in (153.8 x 138.4 cm)
City Art Gallery,
Southampton

Edward Coley Burne-Jones

Birmingham, 1833 –Fulham, London, 1898

The Baleful Head

from *The Earthly Paradise*

1887

Oil on canvas
61 x 51 in
(155 x 130 cm)
Staatsgalerie,
Stuttgart

Luca Giordano

Naples, 1634–1705

Perseus Turning Phineus to Stone

c. 1680

Oil on canvas
112 ½ x 144 in
(285 x 366 cm)
National Gallery,
London

Sebastiano Ricci

Belluno, 1659–
Venice, 1734

Perseus Confronting Phineus with the Head of Medusa

1705–1710

Oil on canvas
25 ¼ x 30 ¼ in
(64 x 77 cm)
J. P. Getty Museum, Malibu

Jean-Marc Nattier
Paris, 1685–1766

Perseus Under the Protection of Minerva Turns Phineus to Stone
1718

Oil on canvas
44 ½ x 57 ½ in
(113.5 x 146 cm)
Musée des Beaux Arts,
Tours

Theseus

Theseus is the great hero of Athens, the son of Aigeus, king of Athens, and of Aithra, the daughter of the king of Troezen. Known to everyone as the hero who killed the Minotaur in the labyrinth built by Daidalos for Minos, the king of the island of Crete, Theseus takes part in many other stories as well, including the killing of the bull of Marathon and the battle between the Lapiths and Centaurs. Helped to kill the Minotaur by Ariadne, a daughter of Minos who was in love with him, Theseus took her with him to Naxos, where he later abandoned her. His exploits are abundantly documented in both Greek art and Roman art. Modern art depicts him as well, most often in connection with Ariadne.

The principal literary source for Theseus is the life written by Plutarch, one of the most prolific authors of antiquity. It is said that this Greek writer, who lived between the 1st and 2nd centuries AD, in his attempt to write history, tried to cleanse the life of Theseus of all its elements of fantasy and improbability, giving us a hero lacking in that "divine splendor" which distinguishes the heroes of the epic poems and ancient tragedies. In Plutarch's telling, Theseus is a historical figure and specific political acts are attributed to him, such as the institution of the Panathenaia festival, the division of society into three classes —the nobles, the artisans, and the farmers—, the minting of money, and the introduction of the democratic process as it was known in classical times. In this way Plutarch aimed to reduce the influence of divine intervention in history, discrediting, for example, some sources that made Theseus the son of Poseidon rather than the son of the Athenian king Aigeus.

Laurent de La Hyre
Paris, 1606–1656

Theseus Finding his Father's Sword
c. 1635–1636

Oil on canvas
55 ½ x 46 ½ in
(141 x 118.5 cm)
Szépmüvészeti Múzeum, Budapest

Theseus and the Minotaur
Roman mosaic
4th century AD
Marble and limestone
161 ½ x 165 ¼ in
(410 x 420 cm)
Kunsthistorisches Museum, Vienna

Another important literary source rich in details about our hero is, again, Apollodorus, who, in a narrative (*Library*, III and Epitome) that is much shorter than Plutarch's, preserves that "divine light" which links the heroes to the mythic sphere of the gods and offers various details omitted by the author of the *Parallel Lives*.

We do not recount here all the deeds of Theseus, which are numerous and quite complicated. We limit ourselves to those episodes most often represented in the history of art. The most popular version of the birth of Theseus is the one according to which Aigeus, the king of Athens, is unable to have a son by his various wives and goes to Delphi to consult the oracle. He does not, however, succeed in understanding the obscure verses uttered by Pythia, the priestess of Apollo, which went more or less like this: "Do not open the neck of a wineskin before you reach Athens." On his way home, Aigeus stopped in Troezen in order to ask the opinion of Pittheus, the king. He, desiring that his daughter Aithra bear a son by Aigeus, and that this son one day become king of Athens, caused Aigeus to get drunk, and then sent his daughter to sleep with him. From this union came Theseus. Aigeus did not want to bring the child with him to Athens, fearing that his nephews, who coveted the throne, would kill him. So he hid his sword and a pair of sandals under a large rock and told Aithra to reveal his identity to the child only when he had become large and strong enough to move the rock. This happened when Theseus was sixteen. Moving the rock, the hero found the objects left by Aigeus and, putting

London Group "B 174"
Active 6th century BC

Theseus and the Minotaur
Amphora
c. 540 BC

Ceramic
h. 16 ½ in
(42.3 cm)
Louvre,
Paris

on the sandals and the sword, which would allow his father to recognize him, he started on his way to Athens. The discovery of the sandals and the sword is depicted on an astonishing Roman terracotta relief from the first century AD (London, the British Museum) that could easily be mistaken for a work of the 15th century. The same scene is the subject of a 17th century painting by the French artist Laurent de la Hyre called *Theseus Uncovers the Arms of his Father Aigeus* (Budapest, Szépmuvészeti Múseum).

On the way to Athens, Theseus had to face traps set by fierce bandits as well as other dangers, all of which were depicted in antiquity but are not found in the art of modern times. On his arrival, Theseus found that all was chaos. Aigeus had organized games in Athens, and Androgeos, the son of Minos, the king of Crete, had been a participant. Androgeos managed to defeat all the other competitors and Aigeus—either from jealousy of the youth's bravery or due to confidence in his strength and courage—sent him to fight the bull of Marathon. Androgeos was killed, and Minos declared war on Athens, defeating her. As tribute, the king of Crete demanded that every nine years Aigeus send seven youths and seven maidens to Crete to be devoured by the dreaded Minotaur, a monster with the body of a man and the head of a bull. The Minotaur was the result of a union between Pasiphae, the wife of Minos, and a bull. Minos had it enclosed in a palace in the form of a labyrinth, designed by the ingenious Daidalos, from which neither the monster nor its victims ever came out. But if anyone were able to kill the

Theseus the Liberator
From the House of Gavius Rufus, Pompeii
50–79 AD

Fresco in 4th style
34 ½ x 38 in
(88 x 97 cm)
National Archeological Museum, Naples

Minotaur with his own hands, and exit the labyrinth, Athens would be liberated from the recurring terrible sacrifice of human life. Arriving in Athens as it was about to send youths and maidens to Crete for the third time, Theseus offered himself, convinced that he could liberate the city from its terrible burden.

Once in Crete, with the help of Ariadne, a daughter of Minos, Theseus succeeded in killing the Minotaur and exiting the labyrinth. Ariadne had fallen in love with Theseus and said that she would tell him how to succeed in his task if he would take her with him to Athens. According to the narrative of Apollodorus, it was Daidalos who suggested to Ariadne that she give Theseus a ball of thread to be attached to the entrance of the labyrinth and that he unwind it as he continued on his way. Then, rewinding it, he would be able to find his way back to the entrance. Because of this, when Minos learned what Daidalos had done, he locked Daidalos and his son Icarus in the labyrinth. To escape, Daidalos then created wings made with wax that he attached to himself and to Icarus, warning his son not to fly too close to the sea or to the sun. But the boy, full of enthusiasm, went too high. The wax melted in the heat of the sun and Icarus fell to his death.

There are many antique amphoras and cups that depict this episode and, from the many possible examples, we mention a black figure amphora with Theseus surrounded by other figures as he kills the Minotaur (Paris, the Louvre). A mosaic from the 4th century AD (Vienna, Kunsthistorisches Museum)

Lord Frederick Leighton
Scarborough, 1830 –London, 1896

Daedalus and Icarus

c. 1869

Oil on canvas
54 ¼ x 41 in
(138.1 x 104.4 cm)
The Faringdon Collection,
Buscot Park

shows us, instead, the killing of the monster in the center of a square labyrinth made of geometrical mazes. Modern art, however, favors other aspects of the legend, and even though there are some depictions of the killing of the Minotaur, the general preference is more for the flight of Daidalos and Icarus and the fatal fall of Icarus, perhaps because, in the eyes of the patrons, these lent themselves more readily to a moral lesson and a warning against imprudence. To mention the name of just one artist, Rubens took up the subject in a painting from 1636, *The Fall of Icarus* (Brussels, Musées Royaux des Beaux-Arts), but there are also examples in ancient art, such as the cameo in the National Archeological Museum in Naples which shows us *Daidalos Making Wings for Icarus* and the fresco in Pompeii (Villa Imperiale, room A) dating to between 20–10 BC also depicting *The Fall of Icarus.*

With the Minotaur dead, Theseus left for Athens, taking Ariadne with him. They stopped on the island of Naxos. According to a version of the story found often in mythology, Theseus abandoned Ariadne on Naxos, while she slept, and returned to Athens alone—perhaps because he was in love with another woman and had brought Ariadne with him only to save her from the anger of Minos. Nevertheless, she did not remain alone for long. The god Dionysus came to Naxos with his merry procession of followers and, charmed by Ariadne's beauty, married her. They had four children together and he took her with him to be among the gods. The Roman author Ovid used this version of the story (*Metamorphoses*, VIII, 172) and added that Dionysus (known

Angelica Kauffmann
Coira, 1741–Rome, 1807

Ariadne Abandoned By Theseus
1782
Oil on canvas
34 ½ x 27 ¾ in
(88 x 70.5 cm)
Gemäldegalerie Alte Meister, Dresden

658

as Bacchus to the Romans) pulled off a crown that she wore on her head and flung it to the heavens, creating one of the constellations. According to the version set down by Apollodorus (*Library*, Epitome), during the time that Theseus and Ariadne stopped in Naxos, she was carried off by Dionysus, who had fallen in love with her, and Theseus returned to Athens disconsolate. It is this episode in the heroic cycle of Theseus that has perhaps had the greatest interest for artists of the modern era. There are many paintings, from the 1500s onward, that depict the meeting of Dionysus and Ariadne on Naxos, with the ship of Theseus in the background as it sails away. The painting by Titian called *The Triumph of Bacchus*, from 1522–23 (London, National Gallery), is one of the most important treatments of this theme in the history of art. As the circle of stars at the top left of the painting leads us to believe, the literary source used by Titian was most likely Ovid.

We conclude this introduction to the heroic cycle of Theseus by relating that when Theseus arrived in Athens with the youths and maidens whose lives he had saved from death at the hands of the Minotaur, he forgot to hoist the white sails that indicate a happy return. The ship still had the same black sails of mourning that it had at the time of its sad departure. Aigeus, believing that his only son and heir was dead, threw himself into the sea (some sources say he flung himself from the top of the Acropolis) and died. This would explain the origin of the name of the Aegean Sea.

Theseus Finding His Father's Arms

Roman bas-relief
1st century AD

Terracotta
c. 22 ½ x 17 in
(57 x 43 cm)
British Museum,
London

"BUT ANGRY AT HIM FOR NOT SACRIFICING THE BULL,
POSEIDON MADE THE ANIMAL SAVAGE,
AND CONTRIVED THAT PASIPHAE SHOULD CONCEIVE A PASSION FOR IT. ...
AND SHE GAVE BIRTH TO ASTERIUS,
WHO WAS CALLED THE MINOTAUR.
HE HAD THE FACE OF A BULL, BUT THE REST OF HIM WAS HUMAN."

(APOLLODORUS, *LIBRARY*, III, 1, 4)

pp. 662–663

Nicolas Poussin
Les Andelys, 1594–Rome, 1665

Jean Lemaire
Dammartin, 1597–Gaillon, 1659

Theseus Finding his Father's Arms
c. 1638

Oil on canvas
38 ½ x 52 ¾ in
(98 x 134 cm)
Musée Condé, Chantilly

The Minotaur
Attic vase
515 BC

Ceramic
h. 5 ½ in, diam. 16 in
(h. 14 cm, diam. 41 cm)
Kunsthandel London (Christie's), London

The Dokimasia Painter

Theseus Killing the Minotaur

Interior of an Attic kylix

480 BC

Ceramic Archeological Museum, Florence

Theseus Killing the Minotaur

From *Les Livres des Histoires*, Ms. Stowe 54, f. 239

15th century

Miniature
c. 7 x 4 in
(18 x 10 cm)
British Library, London

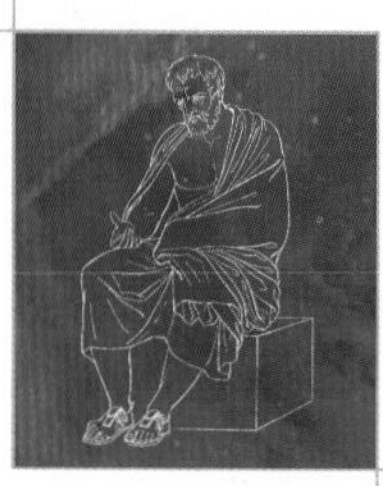

The Fall of Icarus

Late 1st century BC

Fresco
Villa Imperiale,
Pompeii

Icarus and Daedalus with Artemis and Persephone

1st century AD

Cameo
1 ¾ x 1 ¼ in
(4.4 x 3.5 cm)
National Archeological Museum, Naples

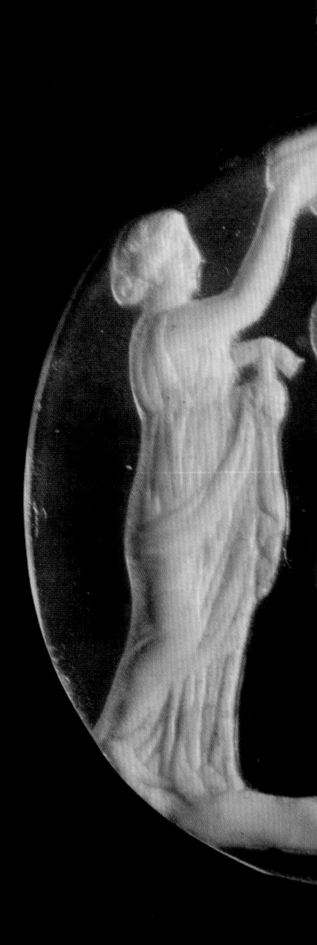

"IN TEDIOUS EXILE NOW TOO LONG DETAINED,
DAEDALUS LANGUISHED FOR HIS NATIVE LAND:
THE SEA FORECLOSED HIS FLIGHT; YET THUS HE SAID:
'THOUGH EARTH AND WATER IN SUBJECTION LAID,
O CRUEL MINOS, THY DOMINION BE,
WE WILL GO THROUGH AIR; FOR SURE THE AIR IS FREE'."

(OVID, *METAMORPHOSES*, VIII)

Daedalus and Icarus
Bas-relief
150 AD

Marble
Villa Albani,
Rome

pp. 678–679

Master of the Campana Cassoni

Active early 16th century

Ariadne Abandoned in Naxos

c. 1510–1515

Oil on panel
27 x 61 in
(69 x 155 cm)
Musée du Petit Palais,
Avignon

Jacob Peter Gouwi

Active early the 17th century

The Fall of Icarus

1636–1637

Oil on panel
76 ¾ x 70 ¾ in (195 x 180 cm)
Prado,
Madrid

Pelagio Palagi
Bologna, 1775–
Turin, 1860

Ariadne Giving Theseus the Thread to Leave the Labyrinth

1814

Oil on canvas
68 ¼ x 105 ½ in
(173.5 x 268 cm)
Galleria Comunale d'Arte Moderna, Bologna

The Argonauts

684

The Argonauts

Lorenzo Costa
Ferrara, c. 1459–Mantua, 1535

The Argonauts
1484–1490

Oil on panel
18 x 33 in
(46 x 33 cm)
Museo Civico, Padua

There is another legend with a plot that is rich with many episodes and characters both human and divine. The Argonauts were heroes and demigods—some fifty in all—who, led by Jason, embarked on a voyage to Colchis in search of the golden fleece. Among the Argonauts were Orpheus, the twins Castor and Pollux (known as the Dioscuri), and Heracles. In his task of obtaining the golden fleece from Aietes, the king of Colchis, Jason was helped by Medea, the king's daughter, who fell in love with him and bore him two children. When Jason left Medea in order to marry Glauke, Medea killed her rival and her own children. There are many mythological episodes that deal with the Argonauts, and figures such as Medea and Orpheus have fascinated artists of all eras—from the ancients to Poussin, and from Canova to Gustave Moreau.

Even though the adventures of the Argonauts are mentioned by Homer, the most complete account of their heroic saga is by the epic poet Apollonius of Rhodes (3rd century BC) in his *Argonautica*. The poem is in four books and very precise in its geography and place names, so that it is possible to reconstruct the itinerary of the heroes as they crossed the Aegean and Ionian Seas, the Black Sea, the Danube River, the Adriatic Sea, the Po River, and the Tyrrhenian Sea, and to recognize the places of their adventures.

The legend is closely tied to the life of Jason, the son of Aison, who was the ruler of Iolkos, in Thessaly. One version of the story tells how the stepbrother of Aison, Pelias, drove

Jason and Pelias
From the House of Fatal Love, Pompeii (or Jason's House)
1st century AD

Fresco
h. 74 ¾ in
(190 cm)
National Archeological Museum, Naples

him from power. Another tells that when Jason was born, Aison made Pelias ruler until Jason reached maturity. But from fear that Pelias would kill Jason in order to hold power, Aison put Jason in the care of the centaur Chiron—the same one who raised Asclepius and Achilles. When he became an adult, Jason presented himself to Pelias in order to claim the throne that was rightfully his. Pelias, who had no intention of giving up the throne, then asked Jason to bring him the golden fleece that the king of Colchis, Aietes, had dedicated to Ares and which was guarded by a terrible dragon. Colchis was on the eastern shore of the Black Sea. Jason hired the architect Argo to build a ship. It had room for fifty oarsmen and was the largest ship ever constructed up to that time. Argo was helped in his work by Athena, who furnished, for the bow, a piece of wood that came from a sacred oak tree, carved by her, and which had the power of speech and the gift of prophesy. The ship was given the name of its builder, Argo, which in Greek means fast. A 1st-century Roman terracotta relief (London, British Museum) shows work on the construction of the Argo under the supervision of Athena. A painting from the end of the 15th century by the Ferrarese painter Lorenzo Costa showing *The Expedition of the Argonauts* (Padua, Museo Civico degli Eremitani) gives us a version of the ship from the 1400s.

During the construction of the Argo, at the suggestion of Chiron, Jason sent heralds all over Greece to invite strong and courageous young men to take part in the expedition. Finally, when the ship was ready and the crew complete, the

Argonauts set sail for Colchis. Even though Apollonius of Rhodes and Apollodorus do not provide the exact same list of heroes and demigods for the crew, some names—and, it could be said, the most important ones—are the same. These include Argo, the designer of the ship; Tiphys, who had learned the art of navigation from Athena; the musician Orpheus; the two sons of Zeus and Leda, Castor and Pollux; Heracles, who left the expedition before its arrival in Colchis; and, obviously, Jason. Before reaching their destination, they had to undergo many trials, such as the battle with the Bebrykes, the liberation of the blind soothsayer Phineus from the curse of the Harpies, the crossing of the Bosphorus into the Black Sea, and the passage through the Symplegades, which were large rocks on the surface of the sea at the entrance to the Hellespont that moved back and forth and that destroyed any ship that dared pass between them.

On his arrival in Colchis, Jason told King Aietes that he intended to bring the golden fleece with him back to Iolkos. Aietes did not want to surrender it, and told Jason that he could take it only if he succeeded by himself in putting a yoke on two bulls which had hoofs of bronze and breathed fire from their nostrils. The two animals, believed impossible to tame, were a gift from Hephaestus. In addition, Jason had to use them to plow a field and then sow it with the teeth of a dragon. Jason was helped by Medea, the daughter of Aietes, who possessed the secrets of various magic potions. The sorceress had been wounded by Eros, the god of love, with one of his arrows, and was in love with Jason. She had

The Lycurgus Painter

Jason and Medea

Apulian volute krater from Ruvo

mid 4th century BC

Ceramic

National Archeological Museum, Naples

Douris

Jason and Athena
Attic kylix
c. 480 BC

Ceramic
diameter 11 ½ in
(29.7 cm)
Museo Gregoriano
Etrusco,
Vatican City

promised to help him if, once the golden fleece had been captured, he would marry her and take her away with him. The promise extracted, Medea gave Jason an ointment with which he covered his entire body and which made him invulnerable to fire and to metal, so that he could subdue the two bulls of Hephaestus. Then, in order to allow him to take possession of the golden fleece, she offered the dragon that guarded it a drink that made it go to sleep. Finally, according to the version by Apollodorus, (*Library*, I, 9), when the Argo was followed by Aietes, Medea killed her own brother, Absyrtus, who had left together with her, by cutting him up and throwing the pieces into the sea one by one. Aietes, who delayed in going after them, did not succeed in catching the Argonauts. In the poem by Apollonius of Rhodes, Absyrtus is sent after the Argo by his father and succeeded in catching the ship at the mouth of the Danube. There, Medea tricked him into going to the temple of Artemis and killed him.

On the voyage back to Iolkos, the heroes again had to confront all sorts of dangers: a storm sent by Zeus, who was angry over the murder of Absyrtus; the bewitching song of the Sirens, which Orpheus, in order to save his companions, countered with a beautiful melody of his own; and the giant Talos, created by Hephaestus at the request of king Minos to protect the island of Crete. Almost all of the various stops made during the voyage have been depicted on ancient vases and reliefs. On the other hand, the artists of the modern era and their patrons have seemed to favor two stories that are

The Myth of Medea
Sarcophagus
Marble
National Archeological Museum of Marche, Ancona

not part of the narrative of the voyage itself but that deal with figures who were, nevertheless, quite important to it: Medea and Orpheus.

Jason and Medea had two children and lived in Corinth. Jason later left Medea in order to marry Glauke, the daughter of Creon, the king. Medea was banished from the city but still had time to plot a terrible revenge. First, she soaked a richly ornamented robe in poison and had it delivered to Glauke by her children. As soon as Glauke put on the robe, she was consumed by fire along with her father, who had rushed to help her. The fire destroyed the entire palace. Medea then killed the children that she had had with Jason and flew to Athens on a wagon drawn by winged horses. This is the version of the story told by Euripides in his tragedy *Medea*.

Perhaps because of its air of mad desperation, it has been taken up by artists of the modern era. Eugène Delacroix, in a painting from 1838 (Lille, Musée des Beaux-Arts), depicted the sorceress just as she was about to kill her children.

The other story concerns the descent of Orpheus into the Underworld. It is filled with pathos, perhaps more than any other story in Greek and Roman mythology. The version in book IV of Virgil's *Georgics* (453–527) is the most detailed and we summarize it here. Pursued by Aristaeus, who wanted to rape her, the nymph Eurydice, the beloved wife of Orpheus, was bitten by a serpent and died. Disconsolate, Orpheus, who was the son of the mortal Oeagrus and the muse Calliope, did not hesitate to embark on a journey to the Underworld, the kingdom of Hades and Persephone, to try to bring

pp. 696–697

The Argonauts
Roman bas-relief
1st century AD

Terracotta
British Museum
London

Master of the City of the Ladies (and scholars)

Orpheus and Eurydice
From *Collected Works of Christine de Pisan*, Ms. Harley 4431, f. 126v
1410–1411

Miniature c. 3 3/4 x 3 in (9.5 x 8 cm), British Library, London

Eurydice back to the world of the living. In order to open the door to the Underworld and to avoid the dangers that it held for anyone who entered, Orpheus made use of all his musical talent. His music and this proof of his love were enough to convince even Hades and Persephone. They allowed him to bring Eurydice back to life on the condition that he not look at her at all until they reached the light above ground. When he had almost reached the land of the living, Orpheus was overcome by doubt that perhaps Hades and Persephone had tricked him, and he turned around. At that instant, Eurydice fell back into the abyss of the Underworld. Orpheus tried to go back a second time, but was not allowed to do so.

Among the many ancient depictions of this tormenting myth is a marble relief from the 4th century BC with *Hermes, Eurydice, and Orpheus* (Naples, National Archeological Museum). In the art of the modern era, are the pair of statues *Orpheus and Eurydice* from 1775–76 by Antonio Canova (Venice, Museo Correr) and the painting *Orpheus at the Tomb of Eurydice* by Gustave Moreau (Paris, Musée Gustave Moreau). In addition, since at least the time of the late Roman Empire, there have been many depictions of Orpheus casting a spell over the animals with his playing and singing, perhaps because of his sorrow over losing Eurydice, as told by Virgil. This can be seen in the 3rd century mosaic *Orpheus Plays Surrounded by the Animals* (Antioch, Museum of Mosaics) and in the painting *Orpheus*, from 1690–1700, attributed to the circle of Jan Brueghel the Elder (Rome, Galleria Borghese).

Herbert James Draper

London, 1864–
London (?), 1920

The Golden Fleece

1904

Oil on canvas
61 x 107 ¼ in
(155 x 272.5 cm)
Cartwright Hall
Art Gallery,
Bradford

698

"IN A LARGE CAULDRON NOW THE MEDICINE BOILS,
COMPOUNDED OF HER LATE-COLLECTED SPOILS,
BLENDING INTO THE MESH THE VARIOUS POWERS
OF WONDER-WORKING JUICES, ROOTS, AND FLOWERS."

(OVID, *METAMORPHOSES*, VII)

Anthony Frederick Sandys
Norwich, 1829–London, 1904

Medea
1866–1868

Oil on panel
24 ½ x 18 ¼ in (62.2 x 46.3 cm)
City Museum and Art Gallery,
Birmingham

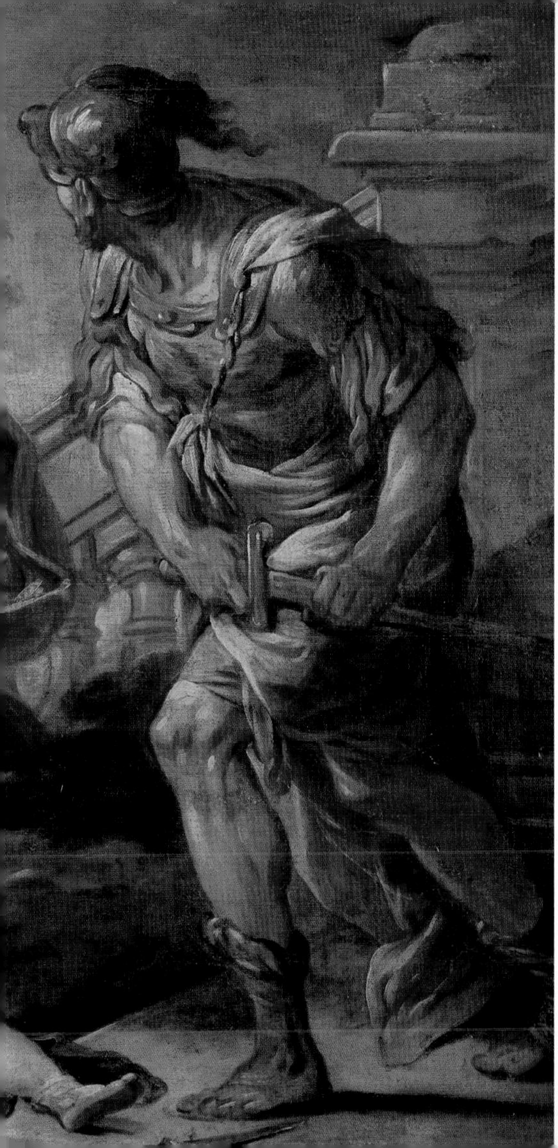

Carle van Loo
Nice, 1705–Paris, 1765

Jason and Medea
1759

Oil on canvas
24 ³⁄₄ x 31 in
(63 x 79 cm)
Musée des Beaux-Arts, Pau

"I WILL NEVER DELIVER UP MY CHILDREN,
HAND THEM OVER TO THEIR ENEMIES, TO BE HUMILIATED.
THEY MUST DIE – THAT'S UNAVOIDABLE, NO MATTER WHAT.
SINCE THAT MUST HAPPEN, THEN THEIR MOTHER,
THE ONE WHO GAVE THEM LIFE, WILL KILL THEM.
AT ALL EVENTS IT'S SETTLED. THERE'S NO WAY OUT..."

(EURIPIDES, *MEDEA*, 1235-1342)

Eugène Delacroix
Charenton-Saint-Maurice, 1798–Paris, 1863

Medea About to Kill her Children

1838

Oil on canvas
102 ¼ x 67 in (260 x 165 cm)
Musée des Beaux Arts,
Lille

Orpheus and the Thracians
Greek vase
c. 450 BC

Ceramic
Staatliche Museen, Antikensammlung, Berlin

“... BY HIS SONGS MOVED STONES AND TREES.
AND WHEN HIS WIFE EURYDICE DIED,
BITTEN BY A SNAKE,
HE WENT DOWN TO HADES,
BEING FAIN TO BRING HER UP,
AND HE PERSUADED PLUTO TO SEND HER UP.”

(APOLLODORUS, *LIBRARY*, I, 3, 2)

Orpheus
Attic vase
410 BC

Ceramic
Regional Archeological Museum,
Syracuse

Orpheus, Isis, and Serapis

Relief of a solar clock face

3rd century AD

Marble
34 ½ x 32 ½
(88 x 83 cm)
Historical District Museum,
Silistra

Orpheus Playing Among the Beasts
From Tarsus
2nd–4th century AD

Roman mosaic
Hatay Museum, Antioch

pp. 714–715

Jan Bruegel the Elder

Brussels, 1568–Antwerp, 1625

Orpheus Charming the Beasts with His Music

1625

Oil on copper
11 ¾ x 15 ¾ in
(30 x 40 cm)
Prado,
Madrid

2876

Albert Cuyp

Dordrecht,
1620–1691

Orpheus Charming the Beasts

c. 1640

Oil on canvas
44 ½ x 65 ¾ in
(113 x 167 cm)
Private collection,
Boston

Jacopo
del Sellaio
Florence, c.
1442–1493

Orpheus Before Pluto and Proserpina
Detail from the
Legend of Orpheus
1490

Oil on panel
Museum of
Western and
Eastern Art,
Kiev

François Perrier

Pontarlier, c. 1590 –Paris, 1650

Orpheus Before Pluto and Proserpina

c. 1647–1650

Oil on canvas
21 ¼ x 27 ½ in
(54 x 70 cm)
Louvre, Paris

Orpheus, Eurydice, and Hermes

2nd century AD

Marble
47 ½ x 35 ½ in (121 x 90 cm)
Louvre,
Paris

ZETVS

Jacopo del Sellaio

Florence, c. 1442–1493

Orpheus and Eurydice

Detail from the Legend of Orpheus

1490

Oil on panel
Museum of Western and Eastern Art, Kiev

724

Jacopo Vignali

Pratovecchio, Arezzo, 1592–Florence, 1664

Orpheus and Eurydice

1625

Oil on canvas
57 ½ x 67 ¾ in
(146 x 172 cm)
Musée de Tessé, Le Mans

Nicolas Poussin

Les Andelys, 1594
–Rome, 1665

Landscape with Orpheus and Eurydice

c. 1650–1653

Oil on canvas
48 ¾ x 78 ¾ in
(124 x 200 cm)
Louvre,
Paris

728

"THEY JUST APPROACHED THE MARGIN OF THE LIGHT,
WHEN HE, MISTRUSTING LEST HER STEPS MIGHT STRAY,
AND GLADSOME OF THE GLYMPSE OF DAWNING DAY,
HIS LONGING EYES, IMPATIENT, BACKWARD CAST
TO CATCH A LOVER'S LOOK, BUT LOOKED HIS LAST.
FOR, INSTANT DYING, SHE AGAIN DESCENDS,
WHILE HE TO EMPTY AIR HIS ARMS EXTENDS."

(OVID, *METAMORPHOSES*, X)

Antonio Canova
Possagno, Treviso, 1757–Venice, 1822

Eurydice
1775

Orpheus
1775–1776

Stone of Vicenza
Eurydice 80 x 21 1/4 x 22 in
(203 x 54 x 56 cm)
Orpheus 80 x 33 1/2 x 21 3/4 in
(203 x 85 x 54 cm)
Museo Correr,
Venice

Jean-Baptiste-Camille Corot

Paris, 1796–Ville-d'Avray, 1875

Orpheus Leading Eurydice from the Underworld

1861

Oil on canvas
44 ¼ x 54 in
(112.3 x 137.1 cm)
Museum of Fine Arts, Houston

732

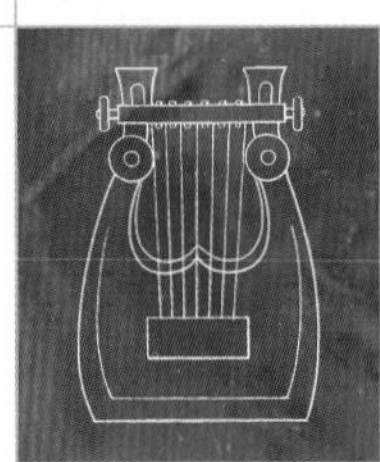

Gustave Moreau
Paris, 1826-1898

Orpheus at the Tomb of Eurydice
1891

Oil on canvas
68 x 50 ¼ in (173 x 128 cm)
Musée Gustave Moreau,
Paris

Luca Giordano
Naples, 1634–1705

The Death of Orpheus

1700

Oil on canvas
31 x 22 ¾ in
(79 x 58 cm)
Musée Hyacinthe Rigaud, Perpignan

The Trojan War

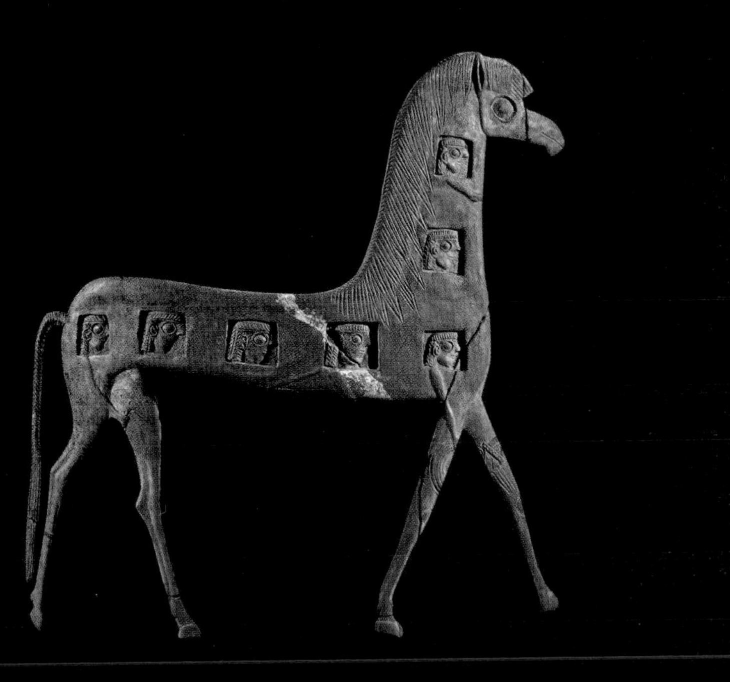

The lives of many heroes play themselves out in the complicated events of the Trojan war, from its remote origins to the surrender of the city as a result of the trick employed by the Greeks with the famous Trojan horse. There are numerous literary sources for the story and between them they present a complete narrative. Even though the central theme of the *Iliad* is in fact the wrath of Achilles and his dispute with Agamemnon, the poem remains the most extensive source describing the conflict. Other sources include the passages in the *Odyssey* that recount the fate of the Greek heroes after the war, the tragedies *Iphigenia in Aulis* and *The Trojans* by Euripides, the accounts provided by Apollodorus in his *Library*, the *Aeneid* by Virgil, and the *Achilleis* by the Roman poet Statius.

We have already spoken about the origins of the Trojan war in the chapter on the gods of Olympus. We can add that this long and bloody war—which archeological excavations and the work of historians have demonstrated actually occurred—is in mythology the battleground on which the gods exercise their power over the destiny of men, involving them in their own quarrels and caprices. Among the gods of Olympus, there are two separate groups, and each clearly helps one or the other of the armies. Aphrodite and Apollo work for the success of the Trojans and support Paris, while Hera and Athena intervene on behalf of the Greeks. Poseidon offers his protection to Aeneas, while Achilles, through his divine mother Thetis, receives his armor from Hephaestus, the blacksmith god.

Paris and Helen

After the 2nd century BC

Marble

c. 15 ¾ x 19 ½ in (40 x 50 cm)

National Archeological Museum, Naples

Helen Arrives at Troy
From *La bouquechardiere di Jean de Courcy*, Ms. Harley 4376, f. 90
c. 1460–1470
Miniature
15 ¾ x 11 ½ in
(40 x 29 cm)
British Library, London

The main character in the Trojan war is, without doubt, Achilles, and a large number of works, in both ancient and modern art, are devoted to him. Among the many legends about the birth and infancy of this hero, we mention the one according to which Thetis, in order to make him invulnerable, held him by his heel and immersed him in the Styx—a river that flowed from a rock in Arcadia and eventually made its way beneath the earth and was, for that reason, considered to be the river of the Underworld. The heel was the only part of Achilles not placed in the miraculous waters and it, therefore, remained vulnerable. This is shown in *Thetis Puts the Child Achilles in the Styx* by Giacomo Franceschini (Genoa, Palazzo Durazzo Pallavicini), in which the figure on the right of a man holding an urn from which water pours out is the personification of the river. In one of the narratives that describes his death, it is an arrow loosed by Paris and guided by Apollo during one of the battles of the Trojan war that wounds Achilles in his vulnerable heel and kills him (Apollodorus, *Library*, Epitome, 5).

After his birth, Achilles was placed in the care of the centaur Chiron, who educated him. Among the many ancient depictions of this subject, is a black-figure vase from around 500 BC with *Peleus Entrusts the Education of the Child Achilles to the Centaur Chiron* (Athens, National Archeological Museum) and the extraordinary 1st century fresco from Herculaneum with *Chiron and Achilles* (Naples, National Archeological Museum). A modern depiction of this theme is seen in a painting by Eugène Delacroix from around

Achilles and the Centaur Chiron
From the Basilica of Herculaneum
45–79 AD
Plaster painted in 4th style
49 ¼ x 50 in (125 x 127 cm)
National Archeological Museum, Naples

1862, *The Education of Achilles* (Los Angeles, J. Paul Getty Museum).

In the narratives, Achilles is presented as a hero able to push back the enemy army all by himself. But when a quarrel arose between him and Agamemnon, the leader of the Greek army, over a woman, Briseis (also known as Hippodameia), Achilles refused to fight, putting the entire campaign in jeopardy. When the dispute was resolved, Achilles returned to the fighting—although, more than anything, it was in order to avenge the death of his beloved friend Patroklos, who had been killed by one of the great Trojan heroes, Hector, the son of king Priam and the brother of Paris, the one responsible for the seduction of Helen. Achilles ended up killing Hector, but, his desire for revenge still not satisfied, he tied the body of his foe to his chariot and dragged it over the ground in front of the tomb of Patroklos for twelve days. Annoyed by this lack of respect for the dead, Apollo complained to Zeus, who commanded Thetis, the mother of Achilles, to put an end to such behavior. When Priam came to request the body of his son, Achilles received him with honor and the two wept together. All these episodes, and many others, are depicted on vases, on reliefs, and on the wall paintings of antiquity. Among so many massacres and so much conflict, however, there are also some scenes of quiet, such as the amphora with Achilles and Ajax playing dice, painted by Exekias between 540 and 530 BC (Vatican City, Museo Gregoriano Etrusco). This is one of the most amazing of all black-figure vases, with a composition that is perfectly balanced, in which

Exekias
Active c. 550–525 BC

Achilles and Ajax Playing Dice
Amphora
c 540–530 BC

Ceramic
h. 24 in (61 cm)
Museo Gregoriano Etrusco,
Vatican City

the seated shapes of the heroes, completely symmetrical, bend forward in an arc and the spears on which they lean, besides being a symbol of their status as warriors, form a triangle that gives balance to the entire image. At the same time, in order to avoid a too rigid symmetry, Exekias presents Achilles with his helmet on his head while the helmet of Ajax leans on the shield behind him, which suggests, among other things, the relaxed nature of the scene.

The *Iliad* ends with a resolution of the quarrel between Achilles and Agamemnon and the return of the body of Hector, with newfound respect for the dead. But the war itself was not over. Its continuation is told in, among other works, the *Odyssey* of Homer. In addition, the narrative of the end of the war and of the tragic defeat of the Trojans forms the beginning of the heroic cycle of Aeneas in Virgil's *Aeneid* (Book II). In more than one of the epic poems, it is said that the idea of declaring an end to the war as a way to achieve victory for the Greeks was a strategy conceived by Odysseus. A gigantic wooden horse, with nine warriors hidden inside its belly and an inscription on it saying that it was dedicated by the Greeks to Athena, was brought close to the walls of the city. At the same time, the Greeks began to burn their tents and pretended to leave camp. Ignoring the prophesies of Cassandra and Laocoon, who had tried to warn the Trojans about danger from the wooden horse, the Trojans brought it inside the city, and with it, their enemies. During the night, Odysseus and his men came out of the horse and opened the gates of the city, which was thus invaded, put to the sword, and burned by the Greeks.

The Horse of Troy
From the book on the *Stories of Troy* by R. Lefebreve
1464

Miniature
Bibliothèque Nationale Française, Paris

This part of the story of the Trojan war has been especially appreciated by artists and, alongside the many depictions of the Trojan horse, from ancient times as well as modern, the brief episode of Laocoon has been very prominent. According to the version told by Virgil (*Aenead*, Book II), this Trojan priest of Apollo launched a javelin at the wooden horse and thereby understood that it was hollow and might be hiding a nasty surprise. While he tried to persuade the Trojans not to trust in it, which they wanted to take as a gift and a sign of the defeat of the Greeks, Athena sent two enormous pythons from the sea and they strangled Laocoon along with his two sons. Two works in particular record this dramatic episode: a sculptural group from the 2nd century BC which shows Laocoon and his sons in a futile attempt to free themselves from the grip of the serpents (Vatican City, Vatican Museums), and the painting *Laocoon* by El Greco from 1610–14 (Washington, D.C., National Gallery of Art) in which, in the background, beyond the elongated bodies gripped by spasms, one sees the wooden horse that was so unwisely brought into the city. Among the most ancient depictions of the Trojan horse, we note a decoration in relief on an amphora from the 7th century BC (Mykonos, Archeological Museum) and a wall painting in Pompeii from the 1st century AD with *The Trojans Celebrate and, Against the Advice of Cassandra, bring the Wooden Horse inside the Walls of the City* (Naples, National Archeological Museum). Among later versions we have *The Building of the Trojan Horse* from around 1538 by Giulio Romano (Mantua, Palazzo Ducale).

Ylyon
La ville de Troye
La porte Dardane

Antonio Canova
Possagno, Treviso, 1757–Venice, 1822

The Abduction of Helen
1798–1799

Tempera on paper
16 ½ x 20 ½ in
(42 x 52.5 cm)
(with the frame)
Gipsoteca Canoviana, Possagno, Treviso

Finally, we cannot close this brief chapter without at least some mention of one other significant figure in art with her own role in the story of Troy. That is Iphigenia, the daughter of Agamemnon and Clytemnestra. As told in the tragedy by Euripides *Iphigenia in Aulis*, and elsewhere, a lack of wind prevented the Greek army from sailing for Troy in order to bring back Helen. It was caused by Artemis (known to the Romans as Diana), who was angry with Agamemnon because he had killed a sacred stag. Then the seer Calchas foretold that the only way to placate the anger of the goddess and bring about favorable winds would be to offer the eldest daughter of Agamemnon, Iphigenia, as a sacrifice. At the end of this dramatic and exciting story, a fawn is sacrificed instead of the girl, and Artemis makes Iphigenia a priestess at her sanctuary in Tauris. We find important depictions of this story on a krater from Puglia from 370 BC (London, British Museum), on a wall painting in Pompeii from the 1st century BC (Naples, National Archeological Museum), and in a spectacular fresco by Giambattista Tiepolo from 1757 (Vicenca, Villa Valmanara).

Sebastiano Ricci

Belluno, 1659–
Venice, 1734

The Abduction of Helen

1708

Oil on canvas
96 x 164 ½ in
(244 x 418 cm)
Galleria Nazionale,
Parma

752

Alessandro
Borel Rogat

Thetis Dipping Achilles in the Styx

1787

Oil on canvas
38 x 53 in
(97 x 135 cm)
Galleria Nazionale,
Parma

pp 756–757

Thetis Giving Achilles into the Care of the Centaur Chiron

Fresco
Palazzo Spada,
Stanza di Achille,
Rome

Pompeo Batoni

Lucca, 1708–Rome, 1787

Achilles and the Centaur Chiron

1746

Oil on canvas
62 ½ x 49 ¾ in (158.5 x 126.5 cm)
Uffizi Gallery, Florence

pp. 760–761

Eugène Delacroix

Charenton-Saint-Maurice, 1798–Paris, 1863

The Education of Achilles

1862

Pastel
12 x 16 ½ in (30.6 x 41.9 cm)
The J. Paul Getty Museum, Malibu

Eug. Delacroix.

Giovanni Battista Tiepolo

Venice, 1696–
Madrid, 1770

Minerva Preventing Achilles from Killing Agamemnon

c. 1757

Fresco
Villa Valmarana,
Vicenza

Felice Giani

San Sebastiano Curone, Alessandria, c. 1758–Rome, 1823

Dispute Between Achilles and Agamemnon

1802–1805

Tempera
Palazzo Milzetti, Faenza (Ravenna)

Claude Lorrain

Chamagne, Nancy, 1600–Rome, 1682

Ulysses Returns Chryseis to her Father

1646

Oil on canvas
46 ¾ x 59 in
(119 x 150 cm)
Louvre,
Paris

Giovanni
Battista Tiepolo

Venice, 1696–
Madrid, 1770

**Thetis
Consoling
Achilles**

c. 1757

Fresco
Villa Valmarana,
Vicenza

Menelaus Holding the Body of Patroclus

Roman copy of a Greek original
150–125 BC

Marble
h. 86 ½ in (220 cm)
Loggia dei Lanzi,
Florence

Priam Supplicating Achilles for the Body of Hector

1st century BC

Silver goblet
h. c. 4 in (10 cm)
Nationalmuseet, Copenhagen

The Funeral of Hector

Relief of a sarcophagus

c. 190–200 AD

Marble

19 ½ x 69 in (50 x 175 cm)

Louvre,

Paris

The Trojan Horse Full with Soldiers

Detail from a relief of an amphora
c. 670 BC

Terracotta
53 in (135 cm)
Archeological Museum, Mykonos

"BROKEN IN WAR AND DISAPPOINTED BY FATE,
WITH SO MANY YEARS ALREADY SLIPPING AWAY,
THE GREEK STAFF CONSTRUCTED A HORSE,
EMPLOYING THE CRAFT OF GODDESS ATHENA.
IT WAS HIGH AS A HILL, AND ITS RIBS
WERE MADE FROM PLANKS OF PINEWOOD.
TO PAY FOR THEIR SAFE RETURN TO GREECE,
THEY PRETENDED: THIS RUMOR GOT AROUND.
BUT, CHOOSING WARRIORS BY LOT,
THEY SECRETELY PUT THEM IN
ON THE BLIND SIDE OF THE HORSE,
UNTIL ITS VAST AND CAVERNOUS BELLY
WAS CRAMMED WITH A PARTY OF ARMED MEN."

(VIRGIL, *AENEID*, II)

Giulio Romano

Rome, c. 1499–Mantua, 1546

The Building of the Trojan Horse

1536–1539

Fresco
Palazzo Ducale,
Mantua

Rhodes sculptors Hagesandros, Athanodoros and Polydoros

Laocoon

1st century AD

Marble
h. 85 ½ in (210 cm)
Musei Vaticani,
Vatican City

El Greco
Candia, 1541–
Toledo, 1614

Laocoon
c. 1610

Oil on canvas
c. 54 x 69 in
(137.5 x 172.5 cm)
National Gallery
of Art,
Washington

782

Massimiliano Benzi Soldani (attributed to)

Florence, 1656–Montevarchi, Arezzo, 1740

The Death of Laocoon

c. 1700

Bronze with golden patina
13 ¾ x 19 ¼ in
(35 x 49 cm)
Private collection

784

Neoptolomos Kills King Priam

6th–5th century BC

Ceramic
British Museum,
London

pp. 790–791

The Sacrifice of Iphigenia
Apulian krater
c. 370 BC

Ceramic
British Museum,
London

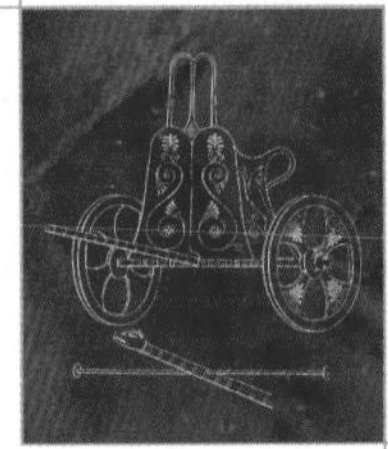

The Fall of Troy
Krater
5th century BC

Ceramic
Museo Nazionale Etrusco di Villa Giulia,
Rome

"BUT AFTER THE ARMY WAS GATHERED AND COME TOGETHER,
WE STILL REMAINED AT AULIS WEATHERBOUND.
IN OUR PERPLEXITY, WE ASKED CALCHAS, THE SEER,
AND HE ANSWERED THAT WE SHOULD
SACRIFICE MY OWN CHILD IPHIGENIA
TO ARTEMIS, WHOSE HOME IS IN THIS LAND,
AND WE WOULD SAIL AND SACK THE PHRYGIANS' CAPITAL
(ONLY IF WE SACRIFICED HER,
BUT IF WE DID NOT, THESE THINGS WOULD NOT HAPPEN)."

(EURIPIDES, *IPHIGENIA IN AULIS*, 87-93)

The Sacrifice of Iphigenia
From Pompeii, House of the Tragic Poet
30 AD

Wall painting
48 ½ x 49 ½ in (123 x 126 cm)
National Archeological Museum, Naples

Richard
van Orley

Brussels, 1663–1723

The Sacrifice of Iphigenia

1702

Miniature on parchment
8 ½ x 7 in
(22 x 18 cm)
Palazzo Pitti,
Galleria Palatina,
Florence

794

Giovanni Battista Tiepolo
Venice, 1696–Madrid, 1770

The Sacrifice of Iphigenia

c. 1757

Fresco
Villa Valmarana, Vicenza

Odysseus

With Troy defeated, some of the Greek heroes returned to their homes and others were sent by fate to distant shores where they founded new cities. The most famous return voyage was that of Odysseus (known to the Romans as Ulysses), the son of Laertes and the king of the island of Ithaca. The narrative of that voyage has come down to us in a literary text of indisputable quality, the *Odyssey* of Homer. The long voyage home of Odysseus, which lasted eight years, is marked by adventure, danger, conflict, and marvelous encounters, in which the hero's cunning is constantly put to the test. On this voyage, between one shipwreck and another, Odysseus must confront the Cyclopes—in particular Polyphemus—, the sorceress Circe, who transformed his companions into swine, and the Sirens. Often, his misfortunes are caused by the imprudence and distraction of his companions and by his own curiosity. For seven years, Odysseus was detained on the island of Ogygia by the nymph Calypso, who wanted to marry him. Nevertheless, the hero was destined to return to his homeland and his wife Penelope, and in this he was helped—just as he was in the Trojan war—by Athena. In the end, Zeus, through the messenger god Hermes, commanded Calypso to let him go.

The voyage of Odysseus is the decorative theme on many ancient Greek vases as well as many Etruscan ones. The art of the modern era has not dedicated as many works to Odysseus as might be expected for a figure of such popularity, especially compared to those for Heracles.

Arnold Böcklin
Basel, 1827–
San Domenico,
Florence, 1901

Odysseus by the Sea
1869

Oil on canvas
18 ½ x 21 ½ in
(47 x 55 cm)
Private collection,
Switzerland

Sebastiano del Piombo
Venice, c. 1485–Rome, 1547

Polyphemus
1512–1513

Fresco
116 x 88 ½ in
(295 x 225 cm)
Villa Farnesina, Loggia di Galatea, Rome

Among the works depicting Odysseus, are his encounter with Nausicaa in the painting *Odysseus and Nausicaa* by Alessandro Allori (Florence, Palazzo Salviati) and *The blind Polyphemus, Seated at the Entrance to his Cave, Feels the Ram under which Odysseus is Hidden*, from 1803 by Johann Heinrich Füssli.

Three episodes from Odysseus' troubled return to Ithaca have had particular appeal to artists. These are, in their sequence in Homer's narrative: the encounter with the Cyclops Polyphemus; his voyage past the island of the Sirens; and the recognition of Odysseus by his old nurse Eurycleia. In the first, at the beginning of the voyage home, Odysseus and his small fleet approach an island—usually identified with Sicily—that has a large number of goats. Odysseus disembarks with twelve of his men, bringing skins filled with wine to be offered to the island's inhabitants. On their way to the interior of the island, they find a cave with a large quantity of milk and cheese. Full of curiosity and against the advice of his companions, Odysseus wants to explore the cave, which was the home of the Cyclops Polyphemus. When this gigantic creature with just one eye in the middle of his forehead returned to the cave and found the intruders, he took them prisoner, blocking the cave entrance with a massive boulder and eating two of the men right away. He intended to eat two more each day, until his human rations were finished. Odysseus then offered the wine that he had brought with him. Polyphemus accepted, drank a large quantity, and, promising Odysseus that he

would eat him last, asked his name. Odysseus answered that his name was "Nobody," which in Greek is *Udeis* and similar in sound to his real name. The clever hero thus obtained time to devise a way to escape with his remaining companions. They could not kill the Cyclops while he slept, because they would then be unable to move the boulder that blocked the cave's entrance. Odysseus decided, therefore, to blind him and with his men drove a large pole, made red hot in the fire, into his only eye. Polyphemus cried for help and called to the other Cyclopes on the island. But when they asked, from outside the cave, who had blinded him, he answered "Nobody." So the other Cyclopes left. Then Polyphemus tried in vain to find his tormentors and moved the boulder away from the entrance to the cave. Odysseus and his men were able to leave the cave by clinging to the underside of the sheep and rams as they went out and thus they escaped the Cyclops. They reached their ships and beat a hasty retreat. The defeat of Polyphemus provoked the anger of his father Poseidon, who as a result placed many obstacles and dangers in front of Odysseus on his voyage home.

Two moments in this story have often been depicted in ancient art: the blinding of Polyphemus and the escape of Odysseus while clinging to the belly of a ram. An ancient, if bitter example, of the first is found on a fragment of a krater from the 7th century BC from Argos (Argos, Archeological Museum). The same theme is seen on a black-figure oinochoe, or jar, from around 500 BC (Paris,

Aristonothos

Polyphemus Blinded by Ulysses and his Companions

Proto-Attic column krater, from Cerveteri

c. 650 BC

Ceramic

h. 14 in (35.8 cm)

Musei Capitolini, Rome

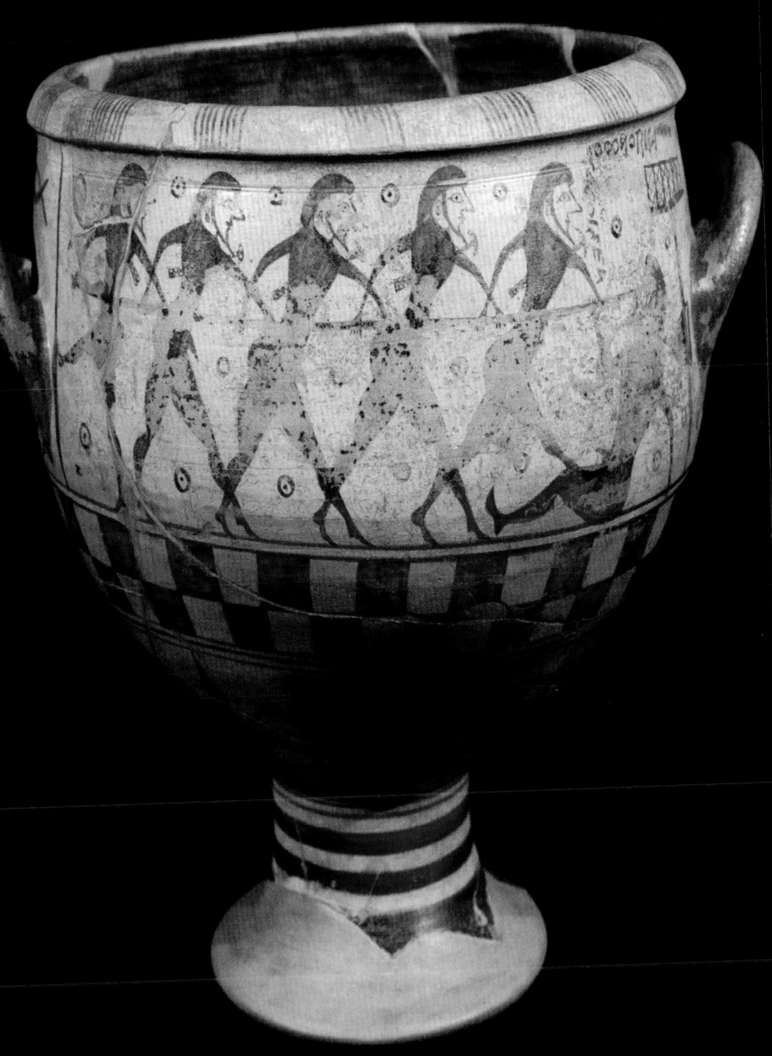

Sappho painter

Odysseus Flees from the Cave of the Cyclops Clinging to the Belly of a Ram

c. 510 BC

Ceramic
h. 13 ¼ in (34 cm)
Badisches Landesmuseum, Karlsruhe

Louvre). A noteworthy example of the second is *Odysseus Flees from the Cave of the Cyclops Clinging to the Belly of a Ram* on a black-figure krater from around the 6th century BC by the Sappho painter (Karlsruhe, Badisches Landesmuseum), a theme that also present in the work by Johann Heinrich Füssli mentioned above.

Among the ancient literary sources, it is in Homer's *Odyssey* that the Sirens are mentioned for the first time. Sea creatures with the head of a woman and the body of a bird, they lived off the coast of the Gulf of Naples and attracted sailors with their enchanting songs in order to kill and devour them. When he was about to pass the island on which they lived, Odysseus, aware of the danger that they posed, commanded his sailors to close their ears with wax. But since he was curious to hear the song of these sea monsters, he did not plug his own ears but instead told his men to tie him to the mast of the ship and not to set him loose under any circumstances until the danger was passed. Thus they were able to sail by the island unharmed.

There are many depictions of this episode in ancient art. One of them, a fine example of a red-figure krater from the 5th century BC, is titled *The Sirens Enchant Odysseus* (London, British Museum). An Etruscan relief from the 2nd century BC (Paris, the Louvre) shows Odysseus tied to the mast of his ship while the boat passes close by the island. We also see Odysseus tied to the mast in a mosaic from the 3rd century AD from Dougga, Tunisia (Tunis, Bardo

Ulysses Blinding the Cyclops
Detail from the Manuscript *L'Epitre d'Othea* by the Master of Epitre
15th century

Miniature
Bibliothèque Nationale de France, Paris

Museum). In more recent depictions, such as the painting *Ulysses and the Sirens* by Herbert James Draper, the sea monsters take the form of creatures half-woman and half-fish—a version of the Sirens that appeared in the Middle Ages, taken out of its mythological context.

When, finally, after twenty years—counting from his departure for Troy until his return to Ithaca—Odysseus comes home, he is practically unrecognizable. He finds his palace invaded by suitors of Penelope who want to take his place as ruler of Ithaca and who consume his wealth with endless banquets. Instead of announcing himself as the master of the house, Odysseus puts on the clothes of a beggar and presents himself at his own palace. He makes himself known only to faithful Eumaios, the head of the swineherds, and to his son, Telemachos, so that he may avenge himself on the suitors. But his nurse Eurycleia, in washing the feet of the stranger before he was presented to Penelope, guessed his identity when she saw a scar that he had received in childhood while hunting a boar. Eurycleia did not reveal the secret to anyone, except Penelope, who found it difficult to believe that the mendicant stranger was her husband.

A red-figure drinking cup with two handles from Attica in the 5th century BC (Chiusi, National Archeological Museum) and a painting from the mid 19th century by the French painter Gustave Boulanger present two interesting illustrations of this episode. The two colors and the fluid

line of the drinking cup are a counterpoint to the scenographic composition of the painting, with its perspective and its modeling according to the accepted canons of the time, along with its academic chiaroscuro. In the painting, we can make out, among others, the figure of Penelope, absorbed in spinning the shroud of Laertes. This is a reference to the strategy that Penelope, the faithful wife of Odysseus, used in order to put off the suitors: she had promised them that she would choose a successor to her husband as soon as the shroud was finished. But every night she would hide and undo the work she had done that day. One painting depicting the attack that Odysseus launched against the suitors who filled his palace deserves particular mention: the great canvas *The Suitors* by Gustave Moreau (Paris, Musée Gustave Moreau).

Johann Heinrich Füssli
Zurich, 1741–London, 1825

Odysseus Between Scylla and Charybdis
1794–1796

Oil on canvas
49 ½ x 39 ¾ in
(126 x 101 cm)
Aargauer Kunsthaus, Aarau

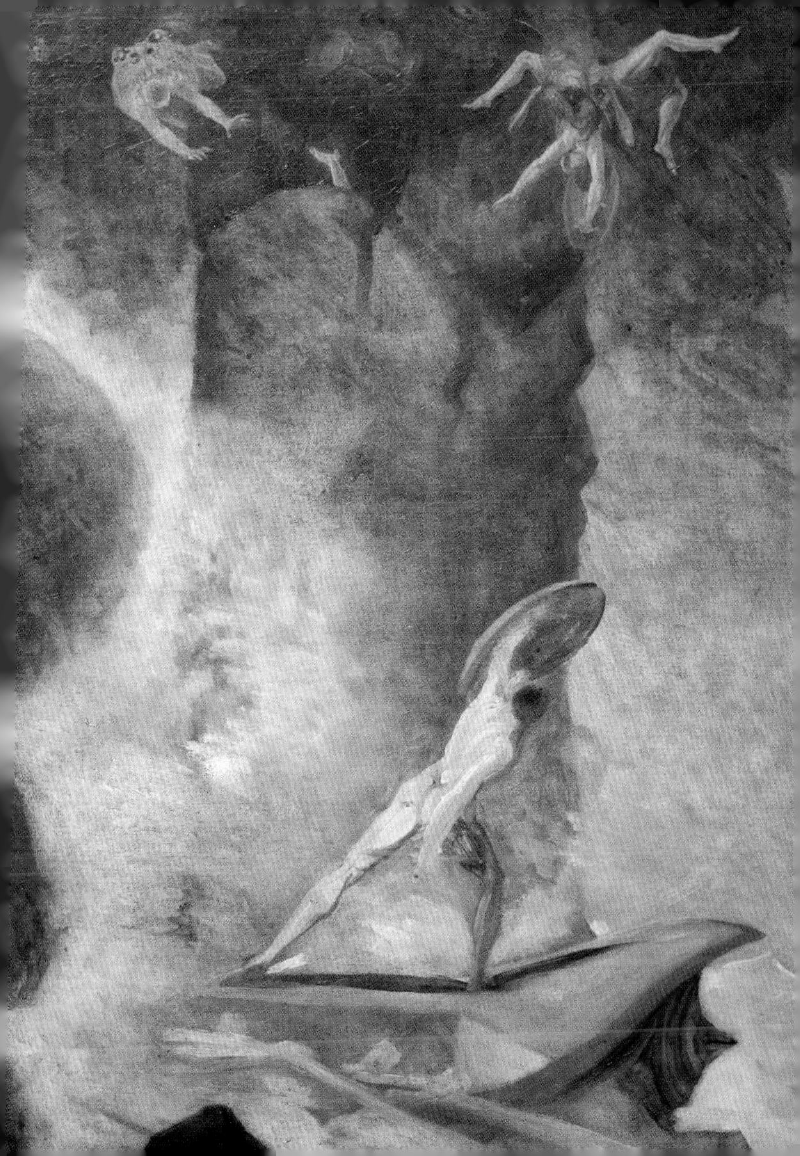

Ulysses Blinding Polyphemus

Vase
Ceramic
Museo Nazionale
di Villa Giulia,
Rome

C. Wilhelm Ernst Dietrich
Weimar, 1712–Dresden, 1774

Ulysses and his Companions Blinding Polyphemus

1760

Oil on canvas
47 ½ x 37 ¼ in (121 x 95 cm)
Anhaltische Gemäldegalerie, Dessau

"A MONSTROUS OGRE,
UNLIKE ANY MAN WHO HAD EVER TASTED BREAD,
HE RESEMBLED RATHER SOME SHAGGY PEAK
IN A MOUNTAIN-RANGE, STANDING OUT CLEAR,
AWAY FROM THE REST."

(HOMER, *ODYSSEY*, IX, 190-193)

Ulysses Giving Wine to Polyphemus

3rd–4th century AD

Roman mosaic
216 ½ x 208 ½ in (550 x 530 cm) (entire)
Villa Romana del Casale, Piazza Armerina,
Enna (Sicily)

Ulysses and his Companions Blinding Polyphemus

Copy of a Greek original by Rhodes sculptors

Mid 1st century BC

Marble
h. 138 in, l. 236 in
(350 cm, 600 cm)
Kunstsammlungen
der Ruhr-Universität,
Bochum

Annibale Carracci

Bologna, 1560–Rome, 1609

The Cyclops Polyphemus

c. 1597–1600

Fresco
Palazzo Farnese,
Rome

pp. 822–823

Joseph Mallord William Turner

London, 1775–1851

Ulysses Deriding Polyphemus

1829

Oil on canvas
52 ¼ x 80 in
(132.5 x 203 cm)
National Gallery,
London

Arnold Böcklin

Basel, 1827–San Domenico, Florence, 1901

Odysseus and Polyphemus

1896

Tempera on panel
27 ¾ x 58 ½ in (65.5 x 148.5 cm)
Private collection

"YOU WILL COME TO THE SIRENS FIRST OF ALL;
THEY BEWITCH ANY MORTAL WHO APPROACHES THEM.
IF A MAN IN IGNORANCE DRAWS TOO CLOSE AND CATCHES THEIR MUSIC,
HE WILL NEVER RETURN TO FIND WIFE AND LITTLE CHILDREN NEAR HIM
AND TO SEE THEIR JOY AT HIS HOMECOMING;
THE HIGH CLEAR TONES OF THE SIRENS WILL BEWITCH HIM.
THEY SIT IN A MEADOW; MEN'S CORPSES LIE HEAPED UP ALL ROUND THEM,
MOLDERING UPON THE BONES AS THE SKIN DECAYS.
YOU MUST ROW PAST THERE; YOU MUST STOP THE EARS OF ALL YOUR CREW
WITH SWEET WAX THAT YOU HAVE KNEADED,
SO THAT NONE OF THE REST MAY HEAR THE SONG.
BUT IF YOU YOURSELF ARE BENT ON HEARING,
THEN GIVE THEM ORDERS TO BIND YOU BOTH HAND AND FOOT
AS YOU STAND UPRIGHT AGAINST THE MAST
...
THUS YOU MAY HEAR THE TWO SIREN'S VOICES AND BE ENRAPTURED."

(HOMER, *ODYSSEY*, XII, 39-52)

Odysseus and the Sirens
Vase from Vulci
c. 480–470 BC

Ceramic
h. 12 ¾ in (32.5 cm)
British Museum,
London

pp. 828–829

Ulysses and the Sirens
Etruscan urn
c. 150 BC

Alabaster
h. c. 11 ¾ in, l. 26 ¼ in (h. 30 cm, l. 67 cm)
Archeological Museum,
Florence

Ulysses and the Sirens
From Dougga
c. 260 AD

Mosaic
51 x 135 ½ in (130 x 344 cm)
Musée National du Bardo
Le Bardo

pp. 832–833

John William Waterhouse

Rome, 1849–St John's Wood, London 1917

Ulysses and the Sirens

1891

Oil on canvas
39 ½ x 79 ½ in (100.6 x 202 cm)
National Gallery of Victoria,
Melbourne

Herbert James Draper

London, 1864-1920

Ulysses and the Sirens

1909

Oil on canvas
69 ½ x 84 in
(176.9 x 213.4 cm)
Ferens Art Gallery, Hull

Scylla
Relief from Melos
5th century BC

Terracotta
British Museum,
London

Pellegrini (Pellegrino Tibaldi)

Puria in Valsolda, Como, 1527–Milan, 1596

Poseidon Opposing the Return of Ulysses

From the Stories of the Ulysses cycle

1554

Fresco
Palazzo Poggi, Bologna

Pellegrini (Pellegrino Tibaldi)

Puria in Valsolda, Como, 1527–Milan, 1596

Ulysses and his Companions Safe after the Storm

From the Stories of the Ulysses cycle

1554

Fresco
Palazzo Poggi, Bologna

Alessandro
Allori

Florence, 1535–1607

Ulysses and Nausicaa

From the Stories of the Ulysses cycle

c. 1575

Fresco
Palazzo Portinari, Florence

Michele Desubleo

Maubege, c. 1602 –Parma, 1676

Odysseus and Nausicaa

c. 1654

Oil on canvas
85 x 106 in
(217 x 270 cm)
National Museum of Capodimonte, Naples

pp. 846–847

Friedrich Preller the Elder

Eisenach 1804–Weimar 1878

Odysseus and Nausicaa

1864

Oil on canvas
National Museum, Graf Raczynski Collection, Poznan

Bartholomäus Spranger

Antwerp, 1546–Prague, 1611

Ulysses and Circe

1580–90

Oil on canvas
43 ¼ x 28 ¼ in (110 x 72 cm)
Kunsthistorisches Museum, Vienna

Pellegrini (Pellegrino Tibaldi)

Puria in Valsolda, Como, 1527–Milan, 1596

Circe changes Ulysses' Companions into Beasts

From the Story of the Ulysses cycle

1554

Fresco

Palazzo Poggi, Bologna

Arnold Böcklin

Basel, 1827–
San Domenico,
Florence, 1901

Odysseus and Kalypso

1883

Tempera on panel
41 x 59 in
(104 x 150 cm)
Kunstmuseum,
Basel

Sienese School

The Return of Ulysses

15th century

Oil on panel
Musée National de la Renaissance,
Ecouen

Gustave Boulanger

Ulysses Recognized by his Nurse Eurycleia

1849

Oil on canvas
57 ½ x 44 ¾ in (146.5 x 113.7 cm)
École des Beaux-Arts,
Paris

"AS OLD EURYCLEIA PASSED HER HANDS
DOWN OVER HIS THIGH
SHE FELT THE SCAR, KNEW WHAT IT WAS,
AND LET THE FOOT FALL AWAY FROM HER.
DOWN WENT HIS LEG INTO THE BASIN,
THE VESSEL OF BRONZE CLANGED AND TILTED,
AND THE WATER SPILT OVER THE GROUND.
JOY AND SORROW SEIZED ON HER HEART AT ONCE,
TEARS WELLED UP IN HER EYES,
AND HER VOICE CHANGED FROM CLEAR TO FAINT.
SHE REACHED HER HAND UP TO HIS CHIN, AND SAID:
'MY OWN DEAR CHILD, YOU ARE ODYSSEUS BEYOND A DOUBT,
YET I DID NOT KNOW YOU FOR MY MASTER
TILL I PASSED MY HANDS ALL OVER YOU'."

(HOMER, *ODYSSEY*, XIX, 467-475)

Ulysses Recognized by his Nurse Eurycleia

Attic skyphos
5th century BC

Ceramic
National Archeological Museum,
Chiusi (Siena)

Giovanni Stradano

Bruges, 1523–Florence, 1605

Penelope at the Loom

1561–1562

Fresco
Palazzo Vecchio, Sala di Penelope, Florence

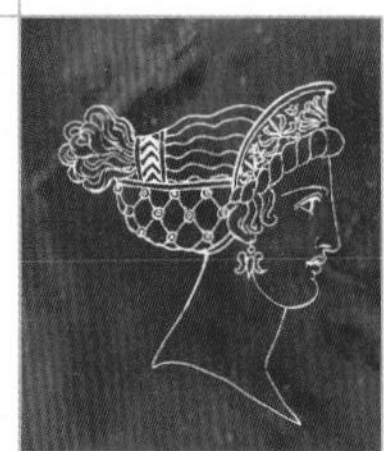

Johann Heinrich Füssli

Zurich, 1741–London, 1825

Penelope Recognizing Ulysses

1803

Oil on canvas
Private collection

Gustave Moreau

Paris, 1826–1898

The Pretenders

1852

Oil on canvas
151 ½ x 135 in
(385 x 343 cm)
Musée Gustave Moreau,
Paris

Oedipus

Although it has been handed down to us above all in the tragedies *Oedipus the King* and *Oedipus at Colonus* written by Sophocles in the 5th century BC, the myth of Oedipus is very ancient and known in many versions. His tragic human experience—to unknowingly kill his father and marry his own mother—is mentioned by Homer in the *Odyssey* and was treated in other epic poems about him, although they have not come down to us. The two other great tragic playwrights, Aeschylus and Euripides, wrote about him in, respectively, *Seven Against Thebes* and *The Phoenician Women*, and Apollodorus took up the story in his *Library* (III, 5). But the version by Sophocles is the one that has been dominant.

Laius, the king of Thebes, and his wife Jocasta shared the same divine origin: both were descended from Cadmus, the founder and first king of Thebes, and the goddess Harmonia. An oracle declared that a son of Laius and Jocasta would kill his father. Nevertheless, according to the narrative of Apollodorus (*Library* III, 5), after becoming drunk, Laius made love to Jocasta and she became pregnant. At the birth of the child, as told in *Oedipus the King*, to avoid the fulfillment of the prophesy, Laius pierced the ankles of the child and passed a rope through them, binding his legs so that he could not walk. He then gave the child to a servant with instructions to abandon him on Mount Cithaeron, thinking that he would not survive. The name Oedipus, in Greek means literally "swollen foot." But the servant did not have the heart to abandon the newborn as he had been

French School

The Finding of Oedipus

17th century

Oil on canvas
48 x 59 in
(121.7 x 150 cm)
Bolton Museum
and Art Gallery,
Bolton

Sphinx of Naxos
From Naxos
c. 570 BC

Marble
h. 91 in (232 cm)
Archeological Museum, Delphi

ordered, and instead gave him to a shepherd from Corinth, who in turn gave him to Polybos and Periboea, the king and queen of Corinth, who did not have any children although they wanted them.

So Oedipus survived and grew up believing himself to be the son of Polybos and Periboea. But one day, during an argument, a man from Corinth turned to him in an offensive way and called him a bastard and a foundling. Oedipus then asked his father for an explanation, as he had never been told that he was adopted. He then decided to leave Corinth in order to consult the oracle at Delphi, which repeated the prophesy and said that he would kill his father and marry his own mother. To avoid this, Oedipus decided not to return to Corinth, as he still believed himself to be the son of the king and queen of that city, and set out for Thebes instead. At exactly that moment, Laius, his real father, full of doubt as to whether his son had actually died and still afraid that the old prophesy might come true, decided to consult the oracle at Delphi. Each ignorant of the identity of the other, the two met on a narrow road. Wounded by the guards who accompanied Laius (or perhaps by Laius himself) because he did not hurry to get out of the way of the carriage of the king of Thebes, Oedipus killed the guards and, unknowingly, his real father.

When Oedipus arrived in Thebes, the city was ruled by Creon, the brother of Jocasta. Creon did not know how to free the city from the Sphinx, which had thrown it in

Painter of Oedipus (attributed to)

Oedipus and the Sphinx
Interior of an Attic kylix, from Vulci
c. 480–470 BC
Ceramic
diam. 10 ¼ in (26.4 cm)
Museo Gregoriano Etrusco, Vatican City

turmoil, and he promised the kingdom of Thebes to anyone who succeeded in defeating it. The Sphinx was a terrible winged monster with the head of a woman and the chest, body, paws, and tail of a lion. It had been sent to Thebes by Hera to punish the city for a crime committed by Laius, who had loved and carried off Chrysippus, the son of Pelops. According to Hesiod (*Theogony*, 326), the Sphinx was the daughter of Echidna and Typhon. In some versions of the story, it sat on a rock on the outskirts of the city, in others it perched on a column. For a long time, the monstrous creature had been asking passersby a riddle, and if they could not answer it correctly, she would devour them. Only the solution to the riddle would free Thebes from this scourge. The riddle was: "What has one voice, and four legs, and two legs, and three legs?" (Apollodorus, *Library*, III, 5). Oepidus was able to give the answer: "Man, who, when born, walks on four legs, then on two legs, and, during old age, uses a cane." The riddle solved, the monster killed herself and the rule of Thebes was given to Oedipus, who, unknowingly, then married his own mother and in this way fulfilled the prophesy.

Among the various stories that deal with the dynasty of Labdacus, who was the father of Laius and the grandfather of Oedipus, the story of the Sphinx is without doubt the most popular one in the history of art. In fact, a great number of ancient sculptures and vase paintings from as far back as at least the 8th century BC are dedicated to it. We see the monster, imposing and solitary, on a fragment

from an Athenian krater of the 7th century BC, and on a marble statue from the 6th century BC (Athens, Museum of the Keramikos). She is also seen as the *Sphinx of Naxos*, from about 560 BC, a statue which stood on a tall Ionic column in front of the temple of Apollo at Delphi (Delphi, Archeological Museum). Among the many depictions of the encounter between Oedipus and the monster is one on the inside of a red-figure cup from the 5th century BC (Vatican City, Vatican Museums), along with a krater from the 5th century BC (Parma, National Museum of Antiquity). Even the art of the modern era has paid homage to this story and two noteworthy examples in painting are *Oedipus and the Sphinx* by Jean-Auguste-Dominque Ingres from 1808 (Paris, the Louvre), and a painting with the same title by Gustave Moreau from 1864 (New York, Metropolitan Museum of Art).

The tragic story of Oedipus continued and Thebes suffered yet another scourge—the infertility of its fields and of its women. The oracle revealed that this disaster occurred because the city didn't do anything to avenge the death of Laius. So Oedipus made every effort to find the guilty one, and decreed that he must be exiled. He did not know that he would be the one to suffer this punishment. When the truth was finally revealed, Jocasta killed herself and Oedipus blinded himself, saying that he was guilty not only of killing his father but of having seen that which was prohibited—referring to sexual relations with his mother. The curse on the dynasty of Labdacus, which was the subject of other tragedies, did not end here, but was visited

Jean-Auguste-Dominique Ingres
Montauban, 1780–Paris, 1867

Oedipus and the Sphinx
1808
Oil on canvas
74 ¼ x 56 ½ in
(189 x 144 cm)
Louvre, Paris

INGRES
1808

Adolf Henning
Berlin, 1809–1900

Oedipus and Antigone
1830

Print
14 x 9 ½ in
(36 x 24 cm)
Archiv für Kunst und Geschichte, Berlin

on the children of Oedipus—Antigone, Eteocles, Polynices, and Ismene.

The works of art in this chapter are not limited to subjects connected to the legends that deal with the descendents of Labdacus. They include other tragic figures such as Orestes, Elektra, Alcestis, Phaedra, and Hippolytos who have been depicted by both ancient and modern artists. For a brief description of their legends and for an understanding of the narrative content of the art, see the brief mythological dictionary at the end of this book.

"FOR HERA SENT THE SPHINX, WHOSE
MOTHER WAS ECHIDNA AND HER FATHER
TYPHON;
AND SHE HAD THE FACE OF A WOMAN,
THE BREAST AND FEET AND TAIL OF A LION,
AND THE WINGS OF A BIRD.
AND HAVING LEARNED A RIDDLE FROM
THE MUSES,
SHE SAT ON MOUNT PHICIUM, AND
PROPOUNDED IT TO THE THEBANS.
AND THE RIDDLE WAS THIS:
'WHAT IS THAT WHICH HAS ONE VOICE AND
YET BECOMES FOUR-FOOTED AND TWO-
FOOTED AND THREE-FOOTED?'.
NOW THE THEBANS WERE IN POSSESSION
OF AN ORACLE
WHICH DECLARED THAT THEY SHOULD BE
RID OF THE SPHINX
WHENEVER THEY HAD READ HER RIDDLE;
SO THEY OFTEN MET AND DISCUSSED
THE ANSWER,
AND WHEN THEY COULD NOT FIND IT
THE SPHINX USED TO SNATCH AWAY ONE OF
THEM AND GOBBLE HIM UP."

(APOLLODORUS, *LIBRARY*, III, 5, 8)

Oedipus and the Sphinx
Calyx krater
5th century BC

Ceramic
h. 16 ½ in
(42,3 cm)
Museo Nazionale
di Antichità,
Parma

Painter of Dareius

Active 340–320 BC

Oedipus and the Sphinx

Apulian krater

4th century BC

Ceramic
h. 56 ½ in
(144 cm)
National
Archeological
Museum,
Naples

880

"CREON MADE PROCLAMATION THAT
TO HIM WHO SHOULD READ THE RIDDLE
HE WOULD GIVE BOTH THE KINGDOM AND
THE WIFE OF LAIUS.
ON HEARING THAT, OEDIPUS FOUND
THE SOLUTION,
DECLARING THAT THE RIDDLE OF THE
SPHINX REFERRED TO MAN;
FOR AS A BABE HE IS FOUR-FOOTED,
GOING ON FOUR LIMBS,
AS AN ADULT HE IS TWO-FOOTED,
AND AS AN OLD MAN HE GETS BESIDES
A THIRD SUPPORT IN A STAFF.
SO THE SPHINX THREW HERSELF FROM THE
CITADEL,
AND OEDIPUS BOTH SUCCEEDED TO THE
KINGDOM
AND UNWITTINGLY MARRIED HIS MOTHER ..."

(APOLLODORUS, *THE LIBRARY*, III, 5, 8)

Gustave Moreau
Paris, 1826–1898

Oedipus and the Sphinx

c. 1888

Oil on canvas
48 ¾ x 36 ½ in
(124 x 93 cm)
La Cour d'Or,
Metz

Fernand Khnopff

Grembergen-lez-Termonde, 1858–Brussels, 1921

The Sphinx

1896

Oil on canvas
19 ¾ x 59 in (50.5 x 150 cm)
Musées Royaux d'Art et d'Histoire,
Brussels

Charles
François
Jalabert

Nîmes, 1819–
Paris, 1901

Oedipus and Antigone

1842

Oil on canvas
45 ¼ x 57 ¾ in
(115 x 147 cm)
Musée des Beaux-Arts,
Marseilles

Painter of the Eumenids

Purification of Oreste by Apollo

Red-figure Krater
c. 380–370 BC

Ceramic
h. 18 in, diam. 20 ½ in (48.70 cm, diam. 52 cm)
Louvre, Paris

888

Berlin Painter

Killing of Aegisthus

Attic red-figure vase

c. 500 BC

Ceramic
h. 13 ¾ in (35 cm)
Kunsthistorisches Museum,
Vienna

ΟΡΕΣΤΕΣ

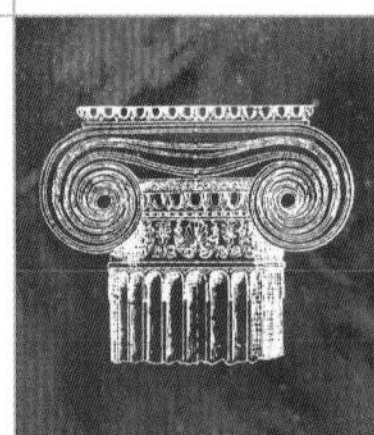

Menelaus

Active 1st century BC–1st century AD

Oreste and Electra

c. 50 BC–50 AD

Marble
Electra (with plinth) h. 75 ½ in (192 cm),
Oreste (with plinth) h. 67 in (170 cm)
Palazzo Altemps,
Rome

Aeneas